WHAT'S MY CHILD THINKING?

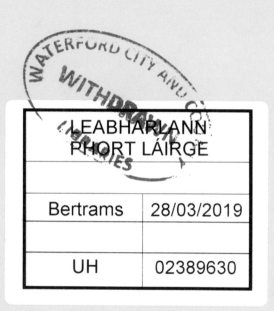

WHAT'S MY CHILD THINKING?

PRACTICAL CHILD PSYCHOLOGY FOR MODERN PARENTS

TANITH CAREY

CLINICAL PSYCHOLOGIST
DR ANGHARAD RUDKIN

DK | Penguin Random House

Senior Editor	Nikki Sims
Senior Art Editor	Emma Forge
Designer	Tom Forge
Editor	Alice Horne
Editorial Assistant	Megan Lea
Illustrator	Mikyung Lee
Producer, Pre-production	Heather Blagden
Senior Producer	Luca Bazzoli
Jacket Designer	Nicola Powling
Jacket Co-ordinator	Lucy Philpott
Creative Technical Support	Tom Morse
Managing Editor	Dawn Henderson
Managing Art Editor	Marianne Markham
Art Director	Maxine Pedliham
Publishing Director	Mary-Clare Jerram

The views expressed in this book are the author's own. If you have any concerns about any aspect of your child's behaviour, health, or wellbeing, it is recommended that you seek professional advice. Neither the author nor the publisher shall be liable or responsible for any loss or damage allegedly arising from any information or suggestion in this book.

First published in Great Britain in 2019 by Dorling Kindersley Limited
80 Strand, London WC2R 0RL

Text copyright © 2019, Tanith Carey

Illustrations copyright © 2019, Mikyung Lee

Copyright © 2019, Dorling Kindersley Limited

A Penguin Random House Company

10 9 8 7 6 5 4 3 2 1 001–310527–May/2019

ISBN 978-0-2413-4380-7

Printed and bound in China
All images © Dorling Kindersley Limited
For further information

see: www.dkimages.com

A WORLD OF IDEAS:
SEE ALL THERE IS TO KNOW
www.dk.com.

Contents

Foreword 8
Introduction 10

1 | WHAT DO YOU WANT FOR YOUR CHILD?

Your own childhood experience 14
What are your values? 16
Putting your child at the centre 18
A "good enough" parent 20

2 | HOW CHILDREN DEVELOP

How children learn 24
Your child's brain 26
Milestones: 2–3 years 28
Milestones: 4–5 years 30
Milestones 6–7 years 32

3 | YOUR 2–3-YEAR-OLD

That's mine 36
Do it myself! 38
No! No! No! 40
No broccoli! 42
Parents' survival guide Eating out 44
Blue cup! No, yellow cup! No, blue cup! 46
Daddy, sit there! 48
No coat! 50
Mummy, don't go! 52
Parents' survival guide Hitting and biting ... 54
Want your phone 56
Just one more 58
Don't like her 60
Parents' survival guide Shyness 62
Let's pretend… 64
I want it now 66
I'm not finished 68
Please, please, please 70
Not Mummy. Want Daddy 72
Parents' survival guide Sleep difficulties 74
Want this story 76
I like this stick 78
What does this one do? 80
One for you, one for me 82
Parents' survival guide Carving out quality time 84
When is tomorrow? 86

④ YOUR 4–5-YEAR-OLD

I want a cuddle **90**

Look what I've done! **92**

I want my dummy! **94**

Are you sad, Mummy? **96**

I'm going to explode **98**

I'm just going to do it **100**

That's so funny **102**

Can Mr Giraffe sit down too? **104**

Parents' survival guide Moving home **106**

I love being with you **108**

Why is the sky blue? **110**

But I didn't hear you **112**

When I was little… **114**

I give up **116**

I'm scared of the dark **118**

I'm telling **120**

Parents' survival guide Car journeys **122**

You love her more **124**

I've lost teddy **126**

You're always too busy **128**

I hate her **130**

I feel sad **132**

I never wanted a little brother **134**

Parents' survival guide Dealing with a
    poorly child **136**

They say I'm a cry baby **138**

I've had a bad dream **140**

I didn't do it **142**

I've had an accident **144**

She's so annoying **146**

I don't want to tidy up **148**

You have to **150**

You can't come to my party **152**

Parents' survival guide Birthday parties **154**

I don't want to **156**

I wet the bed **158**

Will bad people hurt us? **160**

It feels nice **162**

Have I made you sad? **164**

Will you die, too? **166**

You promised **168**

Parents' survival guide Separation and
    divorce **170**

I want it to be perfect **172**

No colouring on the wall **174**

5 | YOUR 6–7-YEAR-OLD

I have to tell you something **178**

It's not fair **180**

I can't do it **182**

I hate you **184**

But Mummy said I could **186**

Parents' survival guide Good manners **188**

No one likes me **190**

They're being mean to me **192**

I wish I had a different family **194**

I don't want to go to school **196**

She's my best friend **198**

Parents' survival guide School pressure **200**

Homework is boring **202**

I'm the best **204**

You're embarrassing me **206**

But all my friends have one **208**

I'm useless **210**

Parents' survival guide Money matters **212**

Stop fighting! **214**

But I'm not tired **216**

I'm bored **218**

I'm not as good as them **220**

I've got a boyfriend **222**

I'm not playing any more! **224**

Parents' survival guide The digital world **226**

Where do babies come from? **228**

Do I have to do music practice? **230**

What's a stranger? **232**

My diary – keep out! **234**

Why do you have to go to work? **236**

You never let me do anything **238**

I want a phone **240**

I'm not pretty enough **242**

Parents' survival guide After-school
   activities **244**

Bibliography **246**

Index **250**

Acknowledgments **256**

Foreword

As a parent, you can often feel as if you should magically know what to "do". Whether your child is refusing to put on a coat or trying to delay bedtime, you can find yourself searching for the "right" words and responses, hoping to stumble across a strategy that works.

We wrote this book to help you know what to do in those moments — by giving you the insight to know what's going on in your child's mind. Drawing on the best research in child psychology and neuroscience, this book will enable you to see the world again as if through your child's eyes — and serve as a reminder of how different that view can be.

But this book is different in one more important way: most parenting books approach interactions with children as a one-way street in which more powerful grown-ups tell children how to behave. Yet parenting has always been a transaction — and it's just as important for us to look inwards. All of us have an internal script that runs through our minds telling us how we "ought" to parent. But unless we listen out for it, we may not recognize that we may be carrying on unhelpful beliefs and biases that stand in the way of really connecting with our children. While genuinely wanting to do our best, we may not realize that what we are saying to impose "discipline" may be making a child who has already lost control more upset. So, this is the first parenting book that simultaneously brings together the thinking of both the parent and the child, so you can navigate more than a hundred real-world interactions and flashpoints.

The ages from 2 to 7 are formative. There is scientific truth behind the Jesuit saying: "Give me the child until the age of seven and I will give you the man." By the age of 7, 90 per cent of brain growth is done and your child's brain will be wired according to the experiences she has had and the kind of care she has received since birth.

Our generation of parents is incredibly fortunate because we know more than ever, thanks to advances in neuroscience, brain scans, and years of research into child development. Working as a team – myself as a parenting author and Dr Angharad Rudkin as a respected child clinical psychologist (with five children between us) – we have set out to distil the best of these findings, much of which have not been easily accessible to parents until now.

We believe no other book has brought parents such a 360-degree view or applied such important research to so many real-world contexts. Of course, no book can cover every eventuality. But we believe that the guidance here can't fail to improve the dance of communication between you and your child.

As parents, we have all had times when we feel like we are lurching from one flare-up, argument, or tantrum to the next. View this book as a translation guide to help you understand what your child is really trying to tell you in these moments, so you can respond more confidently. With this book as your resource, we believe you will have a deeper understanding that will transform your relationship with your child, ultimately helping you both feel calmer and more closely connected.

Tanith Carey

TANITH CAREY

Introduction

What's My Child Thinking? is a new way of looking at the world from a child's point of view – at the same time as considering your own, as a parent. It is designed to help you interpret your child's behaviour quickly and accurately.

On the journey through parenting, there will always be flashpoints. This book is designed to compress the most relevant child psychology, neuroscience, and best practice into grab-and-go sections, so you can access the information you need in the moment. But as well as advice you can use right away, this book also recognizes that some situations need ongoing solutions. So, each scenario also comes with tips on what to do in the longer term.

Tuning into developmental stages

The book covers children from ages 2 to 7 – formative years when children start to explore the wider world, master language, make friends, and assert their independence.

So that you can tune into your child's innermost thoughts whatever their age, the chapters are clearly divided into three main age groups:

- **2–3-year-olds**
- **4–5-year-olds**
- **6–7-year-olds**

to align as closely as possible with key developmental stages. In the same way as you watched as your baby learned to first sit up, then stand, and then walk, the stages of development in the brain (that we can't see) also tend to take place in the same order. That said, each child is unique,

so while these developments may happen roughly consecutively, each child will also go through these stages at his own pace.

A modern approach

Between the ages of 2 and 7, girls' and boys' brains and thinking develop mostly in the same ways. So, while we have used "he" and "she" alternately throughout the book, they are interchangeable. And as gender roles have become more fluid and childcare is no longer seen as primarily the domain of mothers, each scenario will work for a parent of either sex. Although the book talks about mums and dads, it's designed to be useful for anyone who wants to understand children better, whether a grandparent, a teacher, or a carer.

Tapping into the psychology

The book's format of more than 100 everyday scenarios allows you to quickly discover the explanations behind what your child is saying and thinking, while empathizing with a parent's situation and possible feelings.

It's not only children who bombard their parents with a stream of questions every day. Parents themselves often need answers to myriad questions – Should I give into the whining?

" "

A YOUNG CHILD'S PARENTS ARE HIS ENTIRE UNIVERSE. HOW PARENTS TREAT THEIR CHILDREN HAS A DIRECT IMPACT ON HOW THEY FEEL ABOUT THEMSELVES.

Are all screens bad? Why won't he do what he's told? This book delivers the answers to these questions and much more.

The structure of the scenarios allows you to find the information you need fast to resolve whatever situation you find yourself in. By applying the best solution on how to respond, your knowledge of your child and his developmental stage and how to behave in similar scenarios will expand and with this will come a new-found confidence.

Occasionally there are subtly different causes for some kinds of child behaviour, such as tantrums or sibling rows, and each may be better addressed in one of two ways. To this end, flowcharts help you spot how these differ and give you two lots of options on the best way to respond.

Scattered throughout the book are topics that distil the best practice on some of the most common parenting issues – such as eating out, sleep difficulties, and car journeys – into an at-a-glance practical guide, with specific advice for each age group.

A better relationship for both of you

By helping you to interpret your child's behaviour, we hope you will be better able to handle some of the more confusing moments of parenting – and as a result, forge a deeper sense of connection with your child, now, and in the years to come.

CHAPTER 1

What do you want for your child?

Your own childhood experience

Everyone comes to parenting from a unique place, because the starting point is their own childhood. You may continue the type of parenting you received as you feel it worked for you, or you may try to give your child the kind of upbringing you wish you'd had.

To help understand your parenting style, use the following questions as prompts to describe feelings about your childhood; ask any co-parent to do the same. Talk through them or write down your thoughts and then look at your answers together. Don't be surprised if this brings up strong feelings for both of you. Use what you discover to think about your strengths and weaknesses, and work out how best to work as a team for your child.

Q | When it came to conflict, my parents:

◉ rowed in front of me
◉ never argued in front of me
◉ used sniping, sarcasm, or sulking when angry
◉ occasionally argued in front of me, then made up.

Q | When it came to discipline, my parents were:

◉ strict and disciplinarian
◉ relaxed and informal
◉ gave me a balance of love and boundaries.

Q | When it came to schoolwork, my parents:

◉ did not get involved
◉ accepted my results
◉ put me under pressure to achieve.

Q | My bedtimes were:

◉ rigidly enforced
◉ moveable.

Q | As a child, I felt:

◉ my parents had favourites
◉ my siblings and I were treated equally.

Q | When it came to holidays:

◉ family breaks were important
◉ we rarely spent time together as a family.

Q | When it came to expressing feelings:

◉ I was allowed to express my negative emotions
◉ I was encouraged only to express positive ones
◉ my parents did not listen to how I felt.

Q | When it came to material possessions:

◉ I got what I wanted
◉ I only got what I needed
◉ I felt deprived.

Q | When it came to physical affection:

◉ hugs were given freely
◉ I got hugs when I needed them
◉ my parents did not give many cuddles.

A cooperative approach

To add to the mix, it may not only be your wishes that count. If you are raising a family with a partner, there is also the fact that your co-parent will have had a different experience – and bring views of his or her own. If you have a co-parent – whether it's your partner, a former partner, or another family member – you may not realize how much your approaches differ until you talk them through.

Understanding each other's perspectives on parenting beliefs and expectations will not only reduce blame and misunderstanding, but will also help you agree on boundaries for your child that you will be willing to apply consistently.

Doing it on your own

If you are raising your child alone, then you will be in a position to decide how you want to bring your child up. From time to time, though, talk to a trusted friend or family member to help you put any issues you are facing in perspective.

What are your values?

Bringing up children is the most challenging and rewarding role you'll ever have, though it's easier when you are conscious of your own thoughts, attitudes, and beliefs. Discover what matters most to you in terms of values to help guide your parenting journey.

Parenting is also a voyage of discovery. We all set out with the best intentions, determined to create a home full of family harmony. Along the road, you will need patience, kindness, understanding, and every other positive quality you can find. How easy, or not, it is to find these qualities depends on your personal challenges, the ups and downs of your life, and the stresses that crop up. But in order to stay more firmly anchored and not get sucked under by the quicksand of daily life, it's helpful to identify and reinforce your values.

Your parenting mission statement

Values are the things you stand for, the characteristics you want to be remembered for. Crystallizing these values in your mind – and reminding yourself of them – will help you keep being the sort of parent you want to be. Think of them as a job description or mission statement of who you are as a parent.

Such examination of your values needs to be done in conjunction with any co-parent since differences between parents can be deeply confusing to children. Working as a team will also help your child understand what is expected of them and, in turn, make them feel more secure.

WHAT MATTERS MOST TO YOU?

Opposite is a collection of positive qualities, but feel free to add others of your own. Use these values as a basis to answer the questions below. If you have a co-parent, see how your answers compare. When you understand each other's motivations, you will be able to shine a light on where these differences stem from and how you can best meet in the middle.

 For each question below pick out the five values that are most important to you:

- What is important to you as a parent?
- What kind of parent do you aspire to be?
- What sort of relationship would you like to build with your child?
- How would you behave if you were the "ideal you"?
- How would you love to hear people describe your child?
- How would you like your child to describe you later on in life?

clever
free
kind
adventurous
compassionate
strong
polite
conscientious
fit
brave
calm
gentle
mindful
open-minded
determined
honest
PARENTING VALUES
agreeable
sociable
independent
loyal
controlled
smart
balanced
fun to be around
friendly
patient
trustworthy
forgiving
humorous
cuddly
leader
driven
creative
self-aware

Putting your child at the centre

Young children do not yet have the words or life experience to be able to understand or explain their emotions – so they "act" out how they feel. Parenting your child and relating to her with this in mind will benefit her emotional wellbeing no end.

Being a child-centred parent means tuning into your child's feelings and recognizing that they're at a formative stage of development. It's about trying to hear what they are really trying to say, when they act in ways that are inconvenient to grown-ups, rather than branding them "naughty" or "difficult". For instance, if you think of your child as misbehaving, you may rush to think of how to punish her. If you think instead of her as struggling with difficult feelings, your first instinct will be to look for ways to help her through those emotions.

But child-centred parenting is not about "giving in" or letting your child "have her own way". It's about remembering that while you're a fully formed adult, she is still developing and her experiences now will inform the grown-up she will become.

Why empathy is so important
We now know from neuroscience and brain scans that attentive and empathetic parenting affects the way in which a child's emotional brain develops.
⦿ **Better able to deal with life** Children who are parented with empathy when they are upset have been found to fare better at school and handle stress better. This is because when you tune into

your child's feelings and help name them for her, you help build the neural pathways that allow her to regulate her emotions better.
⦿ **A more level temperament** When you comfort your child, you also help calm and regulate her autonomic nervous system. But, if we keep triggering a child's alarm system response with shouting or shaming, believing this is a way to get her to be "good" or "quiet", it can strengthen her primitive fight-or-flight system, making her hypervigilant to threat and more prone to outbursts.

Of course, it's never going to be possible to meet your child's every need all the time. But if you try to relate to her as warmly and empathetically as possible throughout childhood, she is likely to grow up into a warm and empathetic adult as a result.

A parenting crib-sheet
A few basic guidelines can be useful prompts to remind yourself how to behave in any situation:
⦿ **Be a good role model** Children learn most of all by closely watching and imitating their parents. It's probably the single biggest influence on the person they will become. Behave in a way that you would be happy for your child to copy.

AS YOUR GUIDING PRINCIPLE, IT HELPS TO REMEMBER THAT WHAT CHILDREN WANT MOST OF ALL IS TO FEEL UNDERSTOOD BY THE ADULTS WHO CARE FOR THEM.

◉ **Wait for calm** When young children are frightened, frustrated, or angry, it triggers the primal part of their brain – the amygdala, which is wired to respond to threat. This, in turn, leads your child's body and brain to be flooded with stress hormones. At times like this your child won't hear what you have to say. Your first job will be to help her calm her stress response, rather than keep it aroused with overly harsh discipline or shouting.

◉ **Calm yourself, too** When you feel triggered by your child's behaviour, you will also lose your ability to think rationally about what's best to do. If you feel yourself go into fight-or-flight mode, agree to take a moment to step away and regain control before taking your next step.

◉ **Acknowledge your child's negative emotions as well as positive ones** When we hear our children express uncomfortable feelings, such as hatred or sadness, as a loving parent you may often want to talk them out of them or tell them not to feel that way. Be prepared to acknowledge, rather than dismiss, those feelings, so your child can process and deal with them.

A "good enough" parent

Many parents feel the pressure to be "perfect". And in a competitive world, it's easier than ever to feel judged and compared. Yet, although it may sound contradictory, one of the best ways to be a good parent is, in fact, to try not to excel.

This idea – of trying not to be perfect – is the basis of "good enough" parenting – a term first used in the 1950s by the English paediatrician and psychoanalyst Donald Winnicott – and which has gained widespread support from child development experts ever since. It describes how it's more reasonable to aim to meet enough of a child's emotional and physical needs to enable him to grow into a healthy, well-adjusted adult.

Today, we tend to think we have to excel at everything – so "good enough" now tends to sound mediocre or average. However, this is not the case in parenting where being "good enough" is an emotionally healthy approach to a challenging job.

"Good enough" parenting recognizes that we all have our good days and bad days – and that it's better to forgive our mistakes when we make them than dwell on them. Trying to be perfect all the time doesn't help because it's an unattainable ideal for any parent, and creates stress and anxiety. Such an aim also damages the parent–child bond.

When parents don't achieve their goal, Winnicott believed it leads them to become self-critical and lose confidence, when what a child wants most is a happy, relaxed, and loving carer. Trying to be perfect also does not set a good example for children who may grow up with an unrealistic view of what life is like and may pick up perfectionist tendencies. Winnicott also argued that if parents meet a child's need every single time, he'll also never learn what do when he feels bored, sad, or frustrated.

Building parenting confidence

The parenting journey can often feel like you're just getting the hang of a stage of your child's development when things change and you're left running to catch up. But your knowledge of your child – his character, talents, and wants – is ever expanding, which helps to inform the decisions you make in responding to all types of situation. With practice comes confidence.

◀ SEE RELATED TOPICS ▶

What are your values?: pp.16–17
Putting your child at the centre: pp.18–19

" "

THERE IS NO GREATER SECURITY FOR A CHILD THAN TO FEEL CONNECTED TO HIS PARENT.

Time just "being" with your child is precious, so be sure to fit in some every day. At such times, remove all other distractions so you can enjoy each other's company and be in the moment.

Successful parenting relies on open and honest communication between all members of your parenting team. Talk about issues that could turn into resentments, such as sharing childcare jobs, and look for ways to keep stress levels in check.

Enjoy the journey

As well as giving a never-ending supply of unconditional love to your child, learning how to interpret her behaviour and responding with her in mind will lead to a calmer and happier family life.

CHAPTER 2

How children develop

How children learn

Your child's brain started out as a jumbled mass of cells waiting to be wired up. Over time, millions of these neurons have connected and the links between them strengthened by repetition, trial and error, imitation, and problem-solving.

Join your child's learning journey to discover how she gains valuable skills in each of these areas as her brain grows and develops.

Learning about thinking

Your child learns about the world through her senses to start with. When she first put a wooden block in her mouth as a baby, different parts of her brain registered the taste, feel, and weight of it. Later, when she built a tower with that block, she learned about cause and effect, and then gravity, when she repeatedly knocked it over. Every time she did this, neurons fired, forming synaptic connections between her brain cells and thickening her higher-thinking cerebral cortex.

At first, she didn't know the coloured cube she liked so much had a name, because your speech sounded garbled to her. But over time she started to recognize the syllables you said most often when you gave it to her – and worked out it was called a block. As her word bank grew, she started to be able to tap into the power of the left side of her brain to organize her thoughts. This access also allowed her to construct longer sentences – so she could ask more questions and understand your explanation of what was happening around her.

Using more complex sentences, she could start to tell the "stories" of her life experiences to herself – the start of memory formation. With this ability in place, she could now hold on to information, using it to build up her knowledge of the world.

BRAIN CHANGES IN YOUR CHILD'S FIRST SEVEN YEARS ADD UP TO AN UNDERSTANDING OF THE WORLD THAT WILL LAST A LIFETIME.

Learning about relating

As an infant, your child came into the world primed only to get her needs met. Because she knew nothing else, she believed everything centred around her. The circuits for controlling her own emotions were laid down before birth. Over time, though, they were strengthened by "serve and return" interactions: if your child's squeals of delight as you walked into the room have been met with smiles and cuddles, the brain circuits for these emotions were reinforced.

By watching you closely and hearing you talk about your feelings, she gradually worked out that you have emotions, too. When you want her to go to bed, and she wants to stay up, she also discovered that her thoughts and impulses are not the only ones that matter. This understanding, known as "theory of mind", allowed her to see other people's perspectives and form her first friendships.

Learning about feeling

When your child was a baby, she felt just one strong emotion at a time, each originating from the primal, basic part of her brain. Because she had no filter or higher reasoning, it was as if she "became" that emotion. She soon began to realize that certain activities made her happy; the reward centres in her brain released feel-good chemicals – dopamine, oxytocin, and serotonin. But, she also unconsciously recognized that things she didn't want to do made her feel bad; a reaction to the stress hormones adrenaline and cortisol.

As you named your child's feelings for her, and talked about your own, she also learned that there were words to describe how she felt. As the left side of her cortex developed and allowed her to access language, she found she could put her needs into words. The more you spoke to her, the better she could express her feelings.

Your child's brain

To explain the development of a child's brain, many scientists have compared it to a house under construction. Follow this analogy to discover how this amazing organ – with its basic and sophisticated levels – helps mould your child.

When your baby is born, his brain already has its own basic external structure – the walls and the doors – along with all the raw materials it needs to make it spectacular – over 200 billion brain cells. But there's a huge amount of wiring to be done to get it fully up and running.

Building a brain from the foundations up

When he was born, the foundation of your child's brain was also in place. This primitive, lower part – necessary for basic survival and life systems – is also the source of our basic emotions, such as anger and fear. A set of brain structures, collectively known as the limbic system, includes the amygdala – this almond-shaped set of neurons perceives danger, triggering the fight-or-flight response, and plays a key role in the processing of emotions.

As your child grows, the upper floors of his brain are also under construction. This level is where he will do his more sophisticated "higher thinking" – the cerebral cortex; it's the outer layer of the brain and the most recent part to evolve. The cortex includes structures such as the frontal lobes, which are responsible for much of our intelligence, rational thinking, decision-making, and planning.

For the first years, and particularly before the age of 7, this upper floor is a work-in-progress area. Over time, through your child's experiences and interactions, these bottom and top layers link up and start to work together, almost as if there is a staircase between them. This means that gradually your child will gain more control over raw emotions and impulses – that come up from the bottom floor – and learn how to calm them.

Why the left and right sides need to be connected

Throughout childhood, there is another major piece of construction work taking place. Like a double-fronted house, your child's higher brain has a left and a right side. These two hemispheres work very differently, but both have a role to play in an enormous number of functions.

AT TIMES DURING BRAIN DEVELOPMENT, 250,000 NEURONS ARE ADDED EVERY MINUTE.

" "

IN THE FIRST FEW YEARS OF LIFE, THERE ARE MORE THAN 1 MILLION NEW NEURAL CONNECTIONS FORMED EVERY SECOND – A RATE NEVER SEEN AGAIN.

For most people, the left side is where more logical thinking happens as well as the organization of speech and thoughts. The right side registers emotion and recognizes more nuanced verbal and non-verbal communications. These two halves connect via a "corridor" – the corpus callosum.

The most intensive building work on this corridor happens around the age of 2, though it will continue until your child's mid-teens. The wider and bigger this corridor becomes, the more your child is able to freely access both sides of his brain, so he can gradually gain control over his feelings.

Completing the "house"

It won't be until adulthood that your child's "house" is eventually finished – although, there will always be renovations going on. Of course, within these floors, there are many different "rooms" with many different functions. But, if you watch out for how various parts of your child's brain begin to work together, you will start to see how he begins to master his emotions and gain perspective.

Milestones: 2–3 years

Discover what children of this age can do, so that you can relate to them and interpret their behaviour better. Step into their ever-changing world where they will be going through some of the most exciting changes of their lives.

Thinking

The brain is about 80 per cent of its adult size at age 2.

Reasoning, emotions, and memories are all governed by the frontal lobes, which are developing fast.

Skills develop with lightning speed – up to eight new words a day, for example, in speech skills – as connections between brain cells form rapidly.

Imagination takes off as children start to name objects and characters in their world and remember them. There'll be lots of games of "Let's pretend…".

Fascination with cause and effect sees children curious to discover what happens if they push over their block tower or pour water from a jug.

Memory growth means 2-year-olds say "Go swing", for example, before you've even arrived at the playground. By 3, children get excited about seeing people they know and start anticipating Christmas and birthdays.

Improved recall enables children to look forward to seeing the pictures on the following pages of their favourite books, which they enjoy reading over and over.

Relating

Racing ahead with their language mirrors the great steps forward in their walking and running skills.

Able to understand many more words than they can say. Around the age of 2, children have a bank of between 50 and 200 words.

A fast-expanding vocabulary means that by the end of their third year, children know 1,000–2,000 words.

A running commentary is the result of their new-found joy in language. Children describe what they are doing as they play and practise trying out new sounds.

Pronunciation is still improving, but children may make a "t" sound instead of a "k", as in "tate" for "cake", for example. As many as half of their words may be hard to decipher.

Clearer speech and better connections exist between muscles governing speech and their brains. So, by the end of their third year you should be able to understand almost everything your child says.

Feeling

Emotional control lags behind, despite children this age having started to master control of their bodies. This emotional maturity will come as their limbic system (see page 26) continues to develop, a process that will not be fully completed until they reach adulthood.

Extremes of emotions are common until this control develops further. Two- and 3-year-olds can switch between smiling and shrieking in a matter of moments.

Exercising new-found capabilities is seen a lot at this time; children will want to show their growing autonomy with demands such as "Me do it!".

Egocentricity is normal for 2-year-olds. Children may want to be boss but they're also learning the world is a place where not everyone does their bidding – and it's then that tantrums can erupt.

Outbursts are likely to trail off by the age of 3 as children's blossoming vocabulary allows them to start to express verbally how they feel and start to understand the reasons for rules.

Emotional intelligence builds in this phase. Children notice that other people have wants and feelings, too.

Learning how actions affect parents is apparent by 3 – so children are eager to make them happy, although they still feel a strong drive to follow their impulses.

Doing

Rate of growth starts to slow after babyhood. Their limbs are lengthening and their head size becomes more in proportion to the rest of their bodies.

Better coordination results from children's fast-developing nervous systems. And as baby fat turns to muscle, 2-year-olds become much stronger.

Smooth walking and running are now apparent instead of tottering from side to side with legs apart.

Freedom of movement gives children great pleasure; they love spontaneous physical play, such as running down slopes or stopping and starting.

Balance improves, as the right and left sides of the brain better connect, allowing children to skip, hop, and walk along a straight line.

Mastering stairs comes now as children will go from using the same foot each time to using alternate feet.

Refining smaller motions, such as using cutlery to feed themselves, results from developments in fine motor skills; they can already control larger muscle groups.

Drawing skills are starting to emerge. At 2, a child can make lines and rough circles with a crayon grasped in a fist. By 3, many children can grip a pencil between thumb and forefinger using a pincer grip.

YOUR CHILD'S NEW-FOUND LANGUAGE AND MOTOR SKILLS ENABLE HER TO START EXPLORING THE WORLD.

Milestones: 4–5 years

Your child now has a growing awareness of his place in the world, and is starting to test his independence. His chatter will feature plenty of "why" questions and your conversations will have a definite to and fro, which enables you to get more of an idea of his emerging personality.

Thinking

The brain is about 90 per cent of its adult size by age 5.

Attention span, planning, and long-term memory – governed by the prefrontal cortex where there are better connections – are improving. This means children this age can concentrate and play with toys for longer.

Short-term memory gets better – people and events from the recent past are remembered more. They may not yet have a clear understanding of what tomorrow and next week mean. With practice, children can also remember their phone numbers and addresses.

Comparison skills emerge. At this stage, children can sort people and objects in their minds and work out how they are different from other people – and use comparison to talk about those differences.

Categorization of objects, such as fruit, by both colour and size is now possible. Children will take great pride in all their emerging skills.

Understanding more complex sentences follows your child's use of the same. Children also follow two- and three-instruction commands, such as: "Put your toys away, get into your pyjamas and choose a story book".

Relating

With several thousand words at their disposal, children are now better able to carry on more complex two-way conversations.

Speech becomes more fluent as the control of their mouth, tongue, and vocal chords improves; they'll be clearly understood almost all of the time, except when they are upset or very excited. Children can also modulate their tone, for instance speaking in a more babyish voice to children who are younger.

Questioning starts in earnest as children now have the vocabulary to ask questions to find out more about the world. They can also confidently answer questions about themselves from adults.

As children understand the world better, they think it's funny when rules get broken or things don't go to plan. Slapstick, absurdity, and jokes make them laugh a lot.

Friendships are increasingly important to children as they start to work out their identity within peer groups.

Learning social rules means that even though conflicts with friends are inevitable, they will do their best to try to work out a compromise with important playmates.

Feeling

Processing contradictory feelings happens now that they can identify more than one emotion at a time. They can understand it's possible to have two contradictory feelings about the same event – for example to feel happy and sad about the arrival of a new sibling.

Children's "theory of mind" is developing, which means they can now understand others have different feelings and thoughts. However, children this age will test this by telling their first lies.

Pushing boundaries may reflect defiance, though children are still keen to seek their parent's approval, as they test how strictly the rules will be enforced.

Empathy develops as children learn to understand other people's emotions. They will feel sorry about wrongdoings and will realize if their behaviour has upset others.

Children like to feel more in control by practising helping others and being responsible, often role-playing grown-up jobs and wanting to help with household tasks.

Logic will also come into children's thinking and they may like to suggest solutions to problems.

Self-control improves, although they're still impulsive. Because they better express emotions and wants, they are more likely to express anger verbally than physically.

Doing

Balance and coordination has improved, so children this age are able to perform more complex physical moves – hopping and skipping from foot to foot as well as walking along a narrow line.

Speed and agility are on the rise as they run faster and are quick on their feet, allowing them to start and stop quickly, kick a ball hard, and quickly run up stairs.

Muscle strength and dexterity increase, which means they can clamber up anything from climbing frames to trees. Their fine motor skills are now becoming developed enough for them to dress themselves, although shoe-laces and buttons are still problematic.

Holding a pencil with an adult grip is common in most children at this stage. What's more, they will be able to copy a circle, square, and a triangle as well as most of the letters of the alphabet.

More detailed drawings appear as their improved manual dexterity allows them to add more detail to drawings of people, such as mouths, noses, and eyes. Colouring in also becomes neater and nearer the lines.

"

YOUR CHILD IS WORKING OUT HOW TO FIT IN WITH SOCIAL RULES AND IS STARTING TO SEE HOW HIS BEHAVIOUR AFFECTS OTHERS.

Milestones: 6–7 years

By now, you'll probably have a clearer sense of the character your child is becoming, but there are still many developments happening in her brain. Knowing about these can help you support her in her quest for independence, especially outside of the home.

Thinking

The brain has reached adult size. At this age, a child's thinking is now more organized and rational – although they have a long way to go, they show more similarities with adult thinking than differences.

Increased use of logical thinking allows children to start making better sense of how the world works and to understand cause and effect more clearly.

Their more sophisticated understanding also means they will also now recognize that things are not always as simple as they first appear.

Concentration span expands, so that by the end of this phase children are able to concentrate for up to half an hour on new or interesting tasks.

A love of reading starts in earnest now that children can decode words for themselves. They are likely to start enjoying reading books with more complex story lines – and may be happy to read on their own.

A good grasp of numbers means most 7-year-olds will be able to perform simple calculations in their heads. Plus, they can learn to read time from a clock.

Relating

Seeing another point of view is now possible as children's brains, especially the frontal lobes, have developed enough. This allows them to understand that other people have their own thoughts and feelings.

Friendship skills expand as children use knowledge of other's thoughts and feelings to make friends. They are also learning about being tactful.

The effects of peer pressure are felt more than ever. They may want the same clothes or toys as their friends.

Knowing right from wrong is clear now, and children understand that they should follow rules.

Elaborate role-play has overtaken "Let's pretend…" games as children move towards imagining situations that have not happened yet, such as getting married.

Competition strikes as children prefer games with more rules and care about who wins and loses.

Puns and word play delight children now they are more able to understand the double meanings of words; funny jokes and word games are popular.

Feeling

Better regulation of feelings enables children at this age to meet the higher expectations of behaviour from all adults, including teachers.

Privacy may appear as children are starting to realize they can keep their thoughts to themselves. And this applies to their body, too, as they have become aware that their body is different from yours and others' – they may start to want more privacy, preferring to undress on their own or lock the door in the toilet.

More adult-like memories can be laid down now that the prefrontal cortex, which governs attention span, planning, and long-term memory, is developed enough.

Planning is now possible as their higher-order thinking means they can start to see more clearly into the future and plan ahead.

Skills acquisition is recognized now as children want to master skills in order to feel confident. They have learned that being good at things is a confidence boost as well as a social tool.

Comparing themselves with others is common when they start to notice the differences. They begin to compare their abilities, so this is an age when they may start to have their first self-critical thoughts.

Doing

An increasing independence means that the majority of children, for the most part, can wash, dress, and go to the toilet without help.

Refining physical skills happens now that children's core fine and gross motor skills are in place. It's a time when they will want to practise and refine them and often coincides with being keen to learn a musical instrument or develop artistic or crafting skills.

Children's strength and stamina mean that they start to excel at activities – gymnastics, dance, swimming, skateboarding, or sports, such as football.

A certain pride in abilities appears as children understand what they need to do to get better and want to show off their skills to other people.

" "

CHATTY AND SELF-ASSURED, YOUR CHILD IS NOW RECOGNIZABLE AS THE ADULT SHE WILL BECOME.

CHAPTER 3

your

2—3

YEAR-OLD

"That's mine!"

By the age of 2, "mine" is likely to be one of your child's favourite words. However, that doesn't mean that he won't ever be good at sharing. At this early stage, he is just focused on his own wants and he needs adults to teach him this skill.

SCENARIO | **Your child is refusing to share his favourite dinosaur toy with your friend's son at a play date.**

HE SAYS

"That's mine!"

YOU MIGHT THINK

"My friend will think my child is mean and doesn't play nicely."

In his home environment your child will be particularly territorial; he wants control of his things and his space. Children this age are also impulsive. So, he won't be thinking about what will happen when he grabs his dinosaur back. If your child is told he has to hand over his toy to another child, he believes he will never get it back.

It's embarrassing to see your child roughly grab his toy when a small visitor wants to hold it. But the fact he wants to keep it to himself does not reflect badly on your parenting. It may make you wince, but all the toing and froing over a toy is necessary to help him learn how to share.

SHARING IS THE PRECURSOR FOR CONVERSATION SKILLS, PLAYING GAMES, COMPROMISE, RESOLVING CONFLICTS, AND UNDERSTANDING HOW OTHERS FEEL.

WHAT HE'S THINKING

"This is where I live. Everything here belongs to me."

At this egocentric stage, your child is only just learning the concept of ownership. So, it's too early to expect him to share what he's only just discovered belongs to him. While it's good to start helping him learn this skill, it's another year or two before he'll be happy sharing with others.

HOW TO RESPOND

In the moment...

Don't insist Sharing can't be forced. Studies show that children this age are less likely to learn to share if given no choice. If you remove his toy as a punishment, it will increase his worry that others can take away his things, and make him even more possessive. Suggest taking turns instead as it's often easier for young children to accept – you could sing a short song while he waits and then pass the item back when the song is over.

Tell him how others feel Your child will learn how to share better if you talk him through how his visitor might feel. Say: "Joe is happy when you let him play with Mr Rex" or "He's sad when you grab Mr Rex away."

Praise him for sharing When he shares anything with you, make a point of telling him how well he has done – he's more likely to do the same next time.

In the long term...

Be a good sharer yourself One of the most important ways to teach sharing is to be a good role model. When your child's watching, ask to borrow something from your partner for a few minutes and then demonstrate how you say thank you afterwards for letting you have a turn. Make the most of opportunities as they arise, such as sharing a piece of cake or taking turns in a game.

Protect his special things If another child is coming to play, suggest your child puts his favourite toys away and only puts out those he doesn't mind others playing with.

SEE RELATED TOPICS

No! No! No!: pp.40–41
One for you, one for me: pp.82–83

"Do it myself!"

Your toddler is transitioning from a baby who had everything done for her to a young child who wants to do everything for herself. This move to being more independent is natural, no matter how much mess it makes or how much time it takes.

SCENARIO | **Your child insists on pouring her own juice, resulting in several messy spills.**

SHE SAYS

"Do it myself!"

YOU MIGHT THINK

"She's too little to do everything. Why doesn't she just let me help?"

For the first years of your child's life, she was completely dependent on you. Now she is learning that she is an individual, separate from her parents. She now feels ready to assert her independence a bit more and wants lots of practice at activities that have so far been done by adults.

It's natural to feel sad about leaving the baby stage behind, but the associated pride that comes with your child trying and succeeding in new things is a source of joy. It might be hard to resist helping, but all your efforts of restraint will enable her to practise and build her self-worth.

"

ALLOWING CHILDREN TO DO THINGS FOR THEMSELVES HELPS THEM TO BUILD THE SKILLS THEY NEED TO BECOME THEIR OWN PEOPLE.

WHAT SHE'S THINKING

"Even though I keep spilling it, I won't stop and get help from a grown-up."

Mastering a new skill makes your child feel capable. Making a mess is irrelevant compared with how important and proud of herself she feels when she proves to you what she can do. She may get angry and frustrated over early attempts, though.

HOW TO RESPOND

In the moment...

Don't jump in too quickly Resist the temptation to do the task yourself to save time. Intervening too much undermines your child's confidence that she can be independent.

Let her keep trying Even if her first attempt is a disaster, allow her to try again so she learns how to problem solve.

Avoid power struggles If she is not at risk or harming anyone, respect your child's need to be her own boss. If you allow her to assert her independence in acceptable ways, she will become more cooperative.

In the long term...

Value her help Children this age want to help. So, if your child wants to put her plate in the dishwasher or asks to help carry shopping bags, give her a chance and praise her efforts.

Offer smaller steps In their determination to go it alone, children can bite off more than they can chew. Help her build her skills in smaller steps. For example, put her juice in a child-sized jug to pour into her cups, rather than see her struggle with a heavy carton. Next time, offer to help keep her cup steady as she pours.

SEE RELATED TOPICS

Daddy, sit there!: pp.48–49
What does this one do?: pp.80–81

"No! No! No!"

By the age of 2, your toddler is likely to start having temper tantrums. While these outbursts can be intense and unpleasant, they are a normal part of your child's development. Your child is handling this situation the best way he knows how to, and you need to know when to step in to help.

SCENARIO | You need to pop to the shops, but your child refuses to go.

HE SAYS
—
"No! No! No!"

Tantrums are usually due to your child feeling overwhelmed (experiencing high levels of stress and not knowing how to cope) or frustrated (being stopped from doing or getting what he wants). Either way, his higher brain is not developed enough to deal with powerful feelings in any other way.

SEE RELATED TOPICS

No broccoli: pp.42–43
I want it now: pp.66–67

YOU MIGHT THINK

"Why does he have to make such a simple thing so difficult? I don't know what to do."

WHAT HE'S THINKING

"I don't want to go! I want to stay here and play."

Your child's first tantrum may shock and even scare you; embarrassment may feature, too, if it happened in public. When it seems as if all of your requests are met with refusal, exasperation can strike. But these outbursts are not defiance; your child is simply not yet able to express himself.

Whether your child is frustrated or overwhelmed, his outburst is compounded by the fact that he cannot express how he feels effectively in words. A tantrum is the only way he knows to respond to this situation. With time and your help, such outbursts will pass.

HOW TO RESPOND

In the moment...

Put safety first Make sure your child won't get hurt or won't hurt anyone or anything. You may need to clear the area or remove him from the situation.

Stay close and be calm Remain nearby but don't try to talk to, reason with, or make eye contact with your child. If you're calm, it'll be easier for him to calm down too.

Ease towards recovery When the worst passes and your child starts to settle or seek your comfort, then use a soft voice and gentle touch to soothe him and encourage him to respond in a calmer way.

In the long term...

Hold on to reasonable limits Ensure that having a tantrum doesn't become an effective way for your child to get what he wants.

Create predictability and give control Creating routines, offering two choices, and warning of transitions to new activities can avoid future tantrums.

"No broccoli!"

When you first weaned your child onto solids, she would probably happily gobble up most of the foods you fed her. By 2, she's testing her new-found independence by being fussier and may be turning down some of the foods you now offer her.

SCENARIO | **Your child is playing with her food instead of eating it.**

SHE SAYS

"No broccoli!"

Your child is naturally suspicious of new foods and, because her taste is acutely sensitive, some foods may not taste nice. Certain vegetables have flavours that are too intense for her taste buds.

YOU MIGHT THINK

"I spent ages making this meal. She's not getting what she needs. I'm not doing a good job of feeding her."

Because food often represents love in our minds, it can feel like a rejection when a child refuses meals. It's frustrating, too, if you've cooked something especially. Try not to get hung up on what's happened at one mealtime, she'll be getting enough nourishment across the day.

> **" "**
> **BY LEARNING THAT MEALTIMES ARE ALSO AN OPPORTUNITY FOR CHATTING AND TRYING NEW THINGS, CHILDREN LEARN POSITIVE ASSOCIATIONS WITH FOOD.**

In the moment...

Offer less A plate piled high can look daunting, so serve small portions and then offer more when she's finished it. Ask her to try a bit of everything while letting her respond to her feelings of fullness. Never insist on a clean plate. If your child has shifted from eating to just playing, remove the food. The next meal is never far away.

Eat with her Even if you're eating later, sit down and eat a little of the same food. She will get more pleasure from her food if she sees you enjoying it, too.

Stay neutral Keep your praise for eating vegetables low-key. This phase will pass quicker if you don't nag her, get angry, or get upset. Research has found that children eat far more veg when parents don't make a fuss either way.

Avoid bribes Resist offering sweet foods as rewards or threatening to remove treats till she's eaten the vegetables. Otherwise you give her the idea that eating veg is a punishment.

In the long term...

Try, try, and try again Research has found toddlers have to try foods 15 times before they accept them. Keep offering the new foods, alongside foods you know she will eat.

WHAT SHE'S THINKING

"It's great to be boss at mealtimes. And it's funny watching Mummy clear up the food when I drop it."

Your child is in a highly sensory phase and wants to explore new textures – including foods – with her hands as well as make her own choices as she feeds herself. So, she may prefer to squidge the food between her fingers than eat it. Children also play with food because they are little scientists. Dropping food on the floor is watching gravity in action.

SEE RELATED TOPICS
No! No! No!: pp.40–41
Just one more: pp.58–59

Eating out

Eating out is a welcome break from the daily routine of preparing and cleaning up after meals. Restaurants and cafés offer opportunities for kids to practise social skills and understand how to behave in different situations.

Because someone else is doing the cooking, a meal out can be a great opportunity to relax and bond as a family and to chat to your child to make him feel important and included.

Being engaged

While eating out can save you time, it can also be a stressful experience if children don't want to sit still or are noisy around other diners. The reality is that it's a big leap for a young child to go from eating at home to having to be well-mannered and sit still like grown-up for longer times then they are used to. Follow the principles (opposite) to make the best and easiest transitions to relaxed dining as a family.

Be realistic about what your child is ready for and see this chore-free time as a family bonding opportunity to focus on your child, without everyday distractions.

1

Look for family-friendly places
Start with family-style venues or cafés where there is already plenty of noise to drown out any clamour made by your own child, as well as kids' menus and more relaxed and welcoming waiting staff.

4

Clear the table
Young children are curious about new objects. Ask waiting staff to take away any sugar packets, glasses, or condiments that could be grabbed, spilled, or dropped.

6

Choose your timings
When your child is younger, try going after nap-times or go off-peak when there are fewer other customers and the staff will have more time.

9

Select your table with care
Ask for a quiet table in the corner – or a booth – so you won't feel conspicuous if your child is excitable.

GOOD PRACTICE
10 key principles

2
Talk about the rules
Before you go, explain that, just like at home, children will be expected to sit on their chairs, copy grown-up manners, sit properly, and use their "inside", not "outside" shouty voices.

3
Give attention right away
Play games and chat rather than ignore your child when she is quiet or wait for her to get bored. Games such as I-spy can help her understand what's going on around her.

5
Eat one course at a time
If your child is wriggly and only stays in his high chair for 20 minutes, don't expect him to sit through a full meal at a restaurant. Start by just having one course.

7
Notice good behaviour
Praise your child for what he does right, whether it's eating with his mouth closed or using his napkin to keep food off his clothes, so he keeps doing it.

8
Don't resort to your phone
While it might keep your child quiet, handing over your phone will be sending the message that this is the default he can expect to keep him quiet. Your child will also start to associate eating out with screen-time.

10
Model table manners
The best way for children to learn good table manners is to demonstrate them yourself and to eat together as often as possible. Be patient; in time, your child will learn to behave well and eating out will become an enjoyable family time.

2–3 YEAR-OLDS

Let's pretend
Help children learn how restaurants work and how people are expected to behave by playing cafés at home.

Have support
Go with another adult so one of you can take your child for a walk if he gets fractious. Go back and finish the meal if you are not halfway, or call it a day if you are already close to the end.

4–5 YEAR-OLDS

New flavours
Stay safe in restaurants by sticking to favourite foods, but invite your child to try the new tastes on your plate and make it part of the fun.

Cutlery practice
Most children are developing the coordination to hold a knife in an adult pincer grip. Give him the chance to eat like a grown-up.

6–7 YEAR-OLDS

I'll have...
Children of this age are likely to have the confidence to talk to adults they don't know, so let him order his food – it's a good way to practise social skills.

Model politeness
Take the opportunity to explain how important it is to say "please" and "thank you" to waiting staff.

"Blue cup. No, yellow cup. No, blue cup."

At this stage your child is just discovering she has choices – and relishes having her say. But making up her mind when given options is all new. She is normally impulsive and so is also getting used to the idea that she has to live with the decisions she makes.

SCENARIO | Your child can't decide which cup to take with her on a car journey.

SHE SAYS

"Blue cup. No, yellow cup. No, blue cup."

Now that she gets to pick her own things, your child feels she is a big girl. But at this age she doesn't yet know which choice will make her feel better. She is not misbehaving or being fussy; such wavering is a normal part of her development. She needs to know that there is no wrong decision.

YOU MIGHT THINK

"This is taking ages. Why can't she just make up her mind? I had better decide for her."

Decisions are hard to make even when you're a grown-up, so while your child is still getting practice, it may feel to you like she's taking a long time. Resist the temptation to hurry things along by deciding for her. Your patience will be rewarded as her decision-making skills improve.

SEE RELATED TOPICS
No coat: pp. 50–51
I'm not finished: pp.68–69

WHAT SHE'S THINKING

"I can't work out which cup will make me happier."

Having so many choices – and weighing up their pros and cons – whether it's foods, toys, or beakers can feel overwhelming. Such decisions become even harder when your child is stressed or tired. If she is worried – about starting nursery, for example – she is less able to make decisions.

HOW TO RESPOND

In the moment...

Give her the vocabulary Use decision words, such as "choose", "pick", and "prefer", so that she can express how it feels to make a choice.

Put decisions in context It's rare that choices come with a right or wrong answer. Even if she doesn't get the outcome she wanted, she will learn from her mistakes.

Praise her choices When she makes a decision that has been difficult, improve her confidence by reassuring her she has made a good choice.

In the long term...

Narrow the field Too many options are overwhelming for young children. Instead of offering a wide choice, it's often best to present just two options, especially when you are in a rush.

Model decision-making Talk out loud about the decisions you are making throughout the day, whether it's to wear a pair of jeans instead of shorts or cook a baked potato instead of pasta. Let your child hear you weigh up the pros and cons.

"Daddy, sit there!"

Children live in a world where they feel constantly told what to do by grown-ups. Now your child is able to express himself ever more clearly, he is going through a phase of handing out some orders himself.

SCENARIO | **When you have a family meal, your child points to the seat where he wants you to sit.**

HE SAYS

"Daddy, sit there!"

YOU MIGHT THINK

"Aren't we supposed to be the ones in charge?"

Your child believes the world revolves around him. What's more his language development means he is now able to string together sentences of three words, so he can clearly also issue orders. This gives him the chance to see if he can assert his will and find out if you will do his bidding for a change.

You might find it funny, or even cute, that your child is starting to act like a mini-dictator. But then you may worry that if you allow yourself to be bossed about by him, he will turn into a tyrant. Be reassured that his assertiveness is a sign of his growing confidence and speech skills.

❝ ❞

SEE YOUR CHILD'S PERCEIVED 'BOSSINESS' AS A REFLECTION OF HIS GROWING LANGUAGE SKILLS AND NEED FOR HIS WORLD TO FEEL PREDICTABLE.

WHAT HE'S THINKING

"I like things the same. It makes me feel safe."

As your child starts to understand his place in the wider world, it may feel big and scary to him. Predictability makes him feel secure, and he may particularly want the same rituals at transition times, such as meals, because switching from one activity to another is already a big effort.

HOW TO RESPOND

In the moment...

Acknowledge his wish While the decision is ultimately yours, pay attention to and consider his request so he knows you are listening. If you need to sit elsewhere, say: "You're so good with your words now, and I know you like to tell me where to sit, but I am sitting here today to help Mummy bring in the food."

Make light of it Lighten the atmosphere by being humorous. Try rephrasing your child's command as: "So you'd really like it if I sat here today?" and then sit on the floor. Even a young child will appreciate absurdity and seeing the funny side will help him shift his focus.

In the long term...

Don't see it as a battle Take into account that this is a phase. Your child's social and verbal skills are still a work in progress, so he has not yet learnt the diplomacy skills to be polite. He is still learning that other people have thoughts and feelings separate from his own.

Model polite requests Help make "please" and "thank you" part of your child's vocabulary by using it yourself with every request.

Praise your child's flexibility When your child dishes out the orders, and accepts it when you show him his way is not the only way, praise him for showing compromise.

SEE RELATED TOPICS
No broccoli: pp.42–43
Don't like her: pp.60–61

"No coat!"

As children develop the skills to get dressed by themselves and want more independence, they will feel powerful when they can make their own decisions about what to wear. But it can be tricky to know when to let your child decide and when to insist she does what you say.

SCENARIO | **You're off to the park and it's cold outside but your child refuses to put on her coat.**

SHE SAYS

"No coat!"

With all the paraphernalia associated with even a quick trip to the park, extra obstacles to leaving the house can feel like a frustrating step too far. But avoid seeing your child's refusal to wear a coat as a threat to your authority, and instead as a necessary stage of asserting her independence.

YOU MIGHT THINK

"Leaving the house is complicated enough without her being so stubborn. And it's freezing out there."

You may be anxious about her catching a cold or that others won't see you as a good parent if she is not dressed properly, despite your best efforts. But it's useful to know that children often don't feel the temperature as much as adults — they have a smaller skin surface area to keep warm, have a faster metabolism, and are more active, so don't worry too much.

" "

BUILD IN A BIT MORE TIME BEFORE YOUR LEAVE THE HOUSE JUST IN CASE YOUR TODDLER WANTS TO HAVE A GO AT BEING IN CHARGE.

WHAT SHE'S THINKING

"I don't like feeling bundled up. I can't move in this coat."

Just like adults, children also have their favourite clothes. For children, it's often more about comfort and ease of movement. Some coats can make your child feel constricted and certain materials can feel itchy or create unpleasant sensations when close to children's sensitive skin.

SEE RELATED TOPICS
Do it myself: pp.38–39
No! No! No!: pp.40–41

HOW TO RESPOND

In the moment...

Stay calm Rather than shout, get down to her level and speak softly. If you get annoyed, it will turn into a power struggle.

Acknowledge her feelings Tell her: "I can see this is hard for you today. I can help you decide what to wear outside if you like." By allowing her to say what she wants, she is likely to relax. Or offer her the choice of two coats, so she gets her say.

Let your child learn the consequences If it's safe to do so, consider allowing your child to work out for herself how it feels when she is cold. Pack a coat or, as most heat is lost through the head and neck, a scarf and hat may be all she really needs.

In the long term...

Give her choice later In extreme weather, tell her you can't let her choose because today she needs to wear something extra warm. Give her a freer rein when it doesn't matter so much – choosing pyjamas at bedtime. This way you set limits and recognize her choices.

Choose comfortable clothes If you are buying your child a new coat, let her try it on first to check if it feels comfortable. Second-hand clothes are a good option as they have been washed a lot so are softer and not so stiff, as are looser options that she can simply pull over her head herself. Cut out any tags which could annoy your child.

"Mummy, don't go!"

Your child's basic survival instincts mean he is primed to want to stay close to you. When you have to leave him, no matter who he's with, this bond can lead to separation anxiety, which can be very upsetting for both you and your child.

SCENARIO | Grandma has come to look after your child while you nip out for an exercise class, but he clings to you as you leave.

HE SAYS

"Mummy, don't go!"

YOU MIGHT THINK

"I will only be an hour. I feel so guilty when he begs me not to go."

Nothing is quite the same as the love and care a parent gives. Even though by this age, your child knows you continue to exist when you are out of his sight, he is protesting when you leave because you are the person who makes him feel the most safe and loved.

You may feel guilty that you should be at home instead of at the gym. Since young children have finely tuned antennae for your emotions, if you get upset and keep checking on him, the message he gets is: "there is something to worry about when you go" and he will keep protesting.

GIVING YOUR CHILD REGULAR PRACTICE AT BEING WITH OTHERS MEANS HE CAN LEARN TO FEEL COMFORTABLE BEING WITHOUT YOU.

HOW TO RESPOND

In the moment...

(1)

Show faith in your child's carer Your child will take his cues from you, so be confident, smile and engage him and Grandma in a conversation about what games they both like to play and what fun things they will do together. (The same approach would work in a childcare setting.)

(2)

Use distraction Act swiftly to help him shift his focus from his upset feelings to other things. Ask him to engage his curiosity and look around at the toys he can play with and the books he wants Grandma to read with him, for example.

(3)

Avoid lingering farewells Give your child a quick smile and a hug. Tell him you will be back after he's had time for a good play. A confident goodbye will assure him that he will be fine without you.

In the long term...

Practise short separations Build up the time you are apart a little longer each time so your child learns to soothe himself, regulate his feelings, and gets used to be being physically without you. You will both learn that you can survive without each other and the more you practice you get, the less anxious you both will be.

Make parting predictable Saying goodbye will be easier if your farewell is planned and predictable every time. Give your child a hug and two kisses, say, and tell him what you will do together when you return, such as taking a trip to the park, in order to give him something tangible to look forward to.

WHAT HE'S THINKING

"When Mummy leaves, I feel wobbly. I want her here, always."

How your child reacts will depend on how sensitive he is to change and whether he's had sad or happy experiences when you've left him with others before. So far, he has mainly been used to being at home with Mummy or Daddy. So, the challenge of being without you makes him want you as his security even more.

▶ SEE RELATED TOPICS ◀
Don't like her: pp.60–61
Not Mummy. Want Daddy: pp.72–73

Hitting and biting

Though often alarming for parents to witness, aggression between children is a typical part of development. It's usually a phase they grow out of as they learn self-control and the verbal skills to sort conflicts without violence.

Around the age of 2 or 3, your child may bite or hit to release frustration, assert dominance, deal with feelings of being overwhelmed, protect her turf in a war over a toy, or because she feels cornered. Hitting and biting – along with other physical responses such as pinching and kicking – usually happen because your child's higher thinking skills are still developing, so she can't resist her primitive impulses to lash out.

Nevertheless, such behaviour can be a source of anxiety for parents who feel blamed for their child's actions or worry they will be seen as a handful at nursery and not welcome at play dates or parties.

By understanding what's behind such physical aggression and how to respond, you can teach your child different ways of recognizing and dealing with her intense feelings when she feels prone to lashing out.

AGGRESSIVE BEHAVIOUR, SUCH AS BITING AND HITTING, IS A PHASE MANY YOUNG CHILDREN GO THROUGH AS THEY LEARN SELF-CONTROL.

1
Put yourself in your child's shoes
Imagine how you'd react if another adult grabbed one of your most prized possessions and you'll understand how difficult it is for a young child, who still relies a lot on her instincts, not to retaliate when a child takes one of hers.

4
Ask her to use her logical brain
After the incident is over, ask your child to talk through what she could have done differently. This will help use her rational thought processes and gain mastery over her impulsive behaviour.

7
Look for other factors
Your child may be hungry, tired, overwhelmed, or wired from too much sugar but does not yet have the words to express those needs. Give her a consistent routine so flare-ups are less likely to happen.

GOOD PRACTICE

8 key principles

2

Pay more attention to the victim than the hitter

First ask the child on the receiving end if they are OK. This will send a message to your child that she will not be the one to get the attention if she bites or hits.

3

Step in right away

Your child's fight-or-flight reflex has already kicked in by the time she has lashed out. So, rather than shout and elevate her stress levels, remove her, look her in the eye, and say: "No, that's not acceptable. You can be angry, but you mustn't hit."

5

Give positive attention

Children want to be noticed by their parents. If a child feels her parents are not paying attention, she may resort to extreme methods – and hitting is a guaranteed way. To a child, even angry attention is better than nothing at all.

6

Notice kind behaviour

Get into the habit of looking out for the times when she is being kind, sharing, and playing nicely with other children, so she knows this is the way you want her to behave.

8

Give her alternatives

Show your child how to handle a situation differently. When she notices herself getting angry thoughts, suggest that she takes some deep breaths, finds words to say why she's upset, looks for a grown-up, or decides to play with someone else.

TAILORED ADVICE

Age by age

2–3
YEAR-OLDS

No mindreader
Young children may not realize they have to tell other children what they do or don't like when they play. Show her it's OK to express her wishes.

Take it outside
Children are more likely to hit and bite if they are not discharging their energy through lots of physical play.

4–5
YEAR-OLDS

A rewarding solution
If your child is hitting now she's with others more at school, keep a star chart and reward her for the days she uses her hands for helping not hurting.

Practice strategies
Use role-play to help your child think through and practise strategies to avoid physical force.

6–7
YEAR-OLDS

Extra help
If your child has not grown out of hitting, observe her with other children to see if she needs more guidance on how to behave with others.

Is it play-fighting?
Boys tend to engage in more physical rough and tumble, which can leave parents wondering when to intervene. But if all parties are smiling, it's likely to be good-natured.

"Want your phone!"

Thanks to their colourful screens, phones are fascinating to children, so it's easy to understand why you might want to hand yours over when your child is irritable or bored. But for his cognitive and social development, it's best to limit your child's screen-time from an early age.

SCENARIO | While you're waiting for lunch at a café, your child asks if he can play on your phone.

HE SAYS

"Want your phone!"

Whether or not you are on your phone right now, your child will have noticed that adults tend to spend a lot of time on their devices and he wants to be just like you. In your child's eyes, a phone is the ultimate, high-tech toy. If he is allowed to play with it, he will come to see it as the thing he needs to keep him entertained every time.

SEE RELATED TOPICS
I want it now: pp.66–67
What does this one do?: pp.80–81

YOU MIGHT THINK

"My phone will keep him occupied until the food comes. If I say no, he may have a tantrum."

It's tempting to give in to your child rather than face a meltdown. You may also see this as an opportunity to have some time to yourself, or think that a learning app will be good for him. But handing over your phone tells him that gadgets are more interesting than people and that you are happy to give him a substitute for your time and attention.

WHAT HE'S THINKING

"It's fun to play on Daddy's phone. I like the pictures."

The bright colours and graphics that react to the flick of a finger trigger the reward pathways in your child's brain. This instant feedback means that young children would often rather play on phones than play and interact in the real world.

❝ ❞

WHILE YOUR CHILD'S BRAIN IS STILL GROWING FAST, LET IT DEVELOP BY INTERACTING WITH PEOPLE, NOT SCREENS.

HOW TO RESPOND

In the moment...

Keep your phone out of sight Model healthy use of phones, and keep social media checks and phone conversations to a minimum when you are with your child. Children's brains are still hard-wired to learn best from face-to-face interactions.

Say no Be clear that your phone is not on offer here. While it may seem to work miracles to calm down a fractious child, setting clear boundaries on screen use sooner rather than later is the way forward.

Be in the moment Your child is going through enormous cognitive development, so show him that there is plenty to see and talk about around you. Rather than allow him to consume what's on the screen alone, chatting, playing one-on-one games or giving him something to draw are important ways to help practise his evolving language and motor skills.

In the long term...

Don't allow your phone to become his toy If you hand your phone to your child as the default plaything when he's bored, he won't learn to fall back on his own resources, such as using his imagination or showing curiosity about his surroundings.

Don't believe phones will make your child brighter There's no evidence that any phone apps sharpen children's cognitive abilities at this age, but plenty of studies show that a failure to interact and connect with grown-ups at this age contributes to speech and social delays in children.

"Just one more?"

Children would love to be able to choose all the foods they eat, but at this age they are still learning to manage their impulses. As your child takes more control of her eating, she'll be starting to develop a relationship with food that will shape eating habits for life.

SCENARIO | Your child is asking for another cupcake.

SHE SAYS

"Just one more?"

Certain foods are particularly delicious and hard to resist. Eating sweet foods is a strong sensory experience for your child. Children's preference for sweet things is universal and hard-wired from birth, probably to make sure they accept sweet-tasting foods, such as their mother's milk, and to avoid bitter foods that could be poisonous.

SEE RELATED TOPICS

Please, please, please: pp.70–71
No colouring on the wall: pp.174–175

YOU MIGHT THINK

"She's had enough treats. If she goes on like this, I'm worried she is going to get fat."

WHAT SHE'S THINKING

"Why is Mummy not letting me have another one?"

There is no need to worry that your child is being deliberately greedy. She is simply enjoying eating something sweet and does not know where the boundaries are. It's crucial to model a relaxed and stress-free attitude to food. What you say and do informs her learning about food.

Your child will think there's no reason to stop eating cupcakes if they taste yummy. She's not yet tuned into her body's signals that tell her she's had too much sugary food. She needs guidance to start recognizing the clues that relay when she's had enough.

HOW TO RESPOND

In the moment...

Explain why you are saying no Stay neutral while explaining it's important your child eats a good variety of foods to help her grow healthy and strong. While sugary foods can taste yummy, explain she needs room in her tummy for other foods.

Talk about "mouth hunger" versus "tummy hunger" Help your child interpret her appetite signals. Is she hungry in her tummy – or is she hungry for it in her mouth? Frame it as a choice, so she can learn to notice her body's signals and make good decisions herself.

In the long term...

Don't link food with emotions Avoid offering food, and especially sugary treats, as a reward for good behaviour or as a comforter when your child is upset. Suggest a game or activity with you instead.

Buy foods you don't need to restrict Give your child full access to a range of "anytime" healthy snacks that you know she enjoys and which you are relaxed about her eating. If you keep high-fat, high-sugar treats in the house, even if out of reach, she will keep asking for them.

Build structure To make treats less important, have regular mealtimes to sit down and eat together. Any snacks between meals should be eaten at the table, so she is not eating absent-mindedly.

"Don't like her."

Now your child is getting older you may need to put him more into the care of other adults, such as babysitters or nursery staff. However, it may take your child time to trust other adults and to get used to the idea of being looked after by them.

SCENARIO | **Your child says he doesn't want to be left with his childminder, despite being fine yesterday.**

HE SAYS

"Don't like her."

YOU MIGHT THINK

"This is embarrassing. Perhaps I should think of finding another carer."

Your child is programmed to be attached to you and distrust strangers because you are the person most likely to protect him. He may also worry that when you are not with him, you are gone forever. Over time, he'll learn you will always come back.

If you're worried your child is hurting the carer's feelings, you may be tempted to shush him or tell him he likes her really. It can be frustrating and upsetting if he seems to reject all other potential carers.

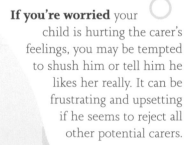

> **IF YOUR CHILD HAS YOU AS HIS SECURE BASE, HE WILL FEEL MORE CONFIDENT BEING CARED FOR BY OTHER PEOPLE.**

WHAT HE'S THINKING

"This person doesn't understand me like Mummy and Daddy do."

At this age, it's normal for children to express their likes and dislikes – and this can change daily. Because your child is still learning others have feelings, he won't yet understand that he can hurt others with his words. Unless there's a real reason for him not to like his carer, he's likely to mean that he prefers you because you make him feel safer.

SEE RELATED TOPICS
Mummy, don't go!: pp.52–53
I want a cuddle: pp.90–91

HOW TO RESPOND

In the moment...

Acknowledge your child's feelings Move your child out of the carer's hearing to reduce both your stress levels. Use brave talk – such as "You are such a strong and brave boy, you can do this" – to tell him you understand it's a challenge to adapt to a new situation.

Reaffirm your confidence in the carer Without dismissing your child's feelings, show him that you trust the childminder and are confident she can look after him, so he feels more confident, too.

Make it clear you'll be back soon Explain where you are going and for how long, using concrete events such as "after lunch" or "before tea", and say you look forward to having special play when you see him again.

In the long term...

Try to understand his discomfort Work out whether your child's objections are due to the difficult transition of saying goodbye or because he does not feel safe and happy there. Leave and stay out of sight to see if he usually settles down.

Fill your carer in Help your child's carer feel confident by giving as much information about your child as possible. See whether the carer wants to know more or takes little interest as this may indicate what they are like with him. While your child will need an adjustment period, if he continues to protest when you drop him off, hides, or becomes withdrawn, you may want to consider whether the arrangement is working.

Shyness

Shy children come into the world generally with more sensitive temperaments. These children may have a slower "take-off" when meeting new people, but over time they can learn how to get used to unfamiliar situations.

Research shows that far from being a problem to "fix", shy children tend to be good observers who are just slower to warm up with new people.

Even *in utero*, the hearts of children who turn out to be temperamentally shy tend to beat faster than those of other babies, scientists have found. This 10 to 20 per cent of infants are born with more aroused nervous systems, which makes them jumpier in new situations.

These may be the babies who are not as quick to smile at strangers and who, as they grow, are more hesitant with people they don't know.

In shy children, it has been found that the brain's antenna for threat – the amygdala – is more easily aroused and triggers more anxious responses. What's more, shy children often grow into thoughtful, empathetic adults who like to listen more than they talk.

1
Avoid the label
If your child hides behind you when you go into a new situation, don't excuse her as "shy" to others. Labelling her as such will sound like it's a negative fixed character trait.

4
Tell her you understand how she feels
Rather than try and force your child out of her shell, show your understanding. You can tell her that you know that sometimes joining in and talking to new people takes practice and in some new situations you feel shy too, but the feeling always eases after you've said a few words.

6
Encourage your child to practise
Explain that like a muscle gets stronger with exercise, social skills improve with practice.

GOOD PRACTICE

8 key principles

2
Reframe shyness
When first meeting your child, other adults may label her shy to explain why she is not friendly. Head off this description by saying she likes to take her time observing new situations first.

3
Prepare her
Your child's worries about being exposed to new situations, such as starting school, will be eased if she knows what to expect. Before starting school or going to a big social event, such as a wedding or party, talk about what it will involve.

5
Teach basic introduction skills
Shyness is only a barrier to forming friendships at first. To help your child work around it, show him how to look friendly when he meets people by smiling, using open body language, and introducing himself by name.

7
Role play
Shy children are particularly worried about saying or doing the wrong thing. Help your child feel more confident by role-playing games with her toys about meeting new people at school or going to a birthday party.

8
Be a good role model
Mirror neurons in your child's brain help her to learn social skills by watching you and other caregivers and copying what you do. Set a good example by being friendly to new people and showing good manners and consideration for others.

TAILORED ADVICE

Age by age

2–3 YEAR-OLDS

Their secure base
At this stage, introduce your child from the safety of your arms (or your lap) so she can observe and get used to her surroundings first.

Worry-free separation
Follow the steps on page 52 to ease separation anxiety and any clinginess if your child starts to be looked after more by other people.

4–5 YEAR-OLDS

Practice sessions
Look out for opportunities for your child to fine-tune her social skills, such as talking to relatives on the phone, paying in a shop, and saying please and thank you to strangers.

To and fro
Now your child is meeting new children at school, show her how to respond to friendly overtures by asking questions back and learning how to join in games.

6–7 YEAR-OLDS

Set up play dates
Your child is likely to feel more confident and outgoing with other children in her home territory.

Follow her passions
Look for an activity based on your child's natural "spark". She will join others who she already has a lot in common.

"Let's pretend..."

By the age of 2, pretend play is a key part of your child's development: it allows him to show his curiosity, solve problems, comprehend people and their actions, and improve his social skills. If your child invites you into his make-believe world, do accept and follow his lead.

SCENARIO | Your child says he wants to play cafés with you.

HE SAYS

"Let's pretend..."

YOU MIGHT THINK

"Not again! How long will this go on for, today?"

In your child's mind, he's taking on the persona of café owner. He'll relish being in charge and directing you to be a character, playing by his rules. In doing so, he is improving his emerging social skills and boosting his cognitive development by using information from the world around him.

While children love to play make-believe, such games can feel repetitive to many adults. But if your child asks you to take part, then join in and be patient. The more you embrace these opportunities of engaging with your child, the more you get to know him and the more fun you can have together.

PRETEND PLAY ALLOWS CHILDREN TO LEARN SKILLS THEY CAN TRANSFER TO THE REAL WORLD – MAKING FRIENDS, PROBLEM-SOLVING, AND SELF-EXPRESSION.

WHAT HE'S THINKING

"You've got to play along, too!"

Joining in a game that your toddler has dreamed up will make him feel loved and valued. Because every aspect of the café is real to him and he's in charge, there's no doubt in his mind that your character is integral to the game.

HOW TO RESPOND

In the moment…

Be present Put all thoughts of other jobs out of your mind and leave your phone in another room. It's worth devoting this short time – 10–15 minutes, say – because of the benefits for your child.

Let him make the rules If you give your child control over his make-believe world, his need for power is met and he is less likely to want to take charge in other areas of life, such as at mealtimes. His behaviour is likely to improve as a result.

Wind it down Rather than abruptly saying the game is over, give your toddler a warning, and then a reminder, that you will need to finish in a few minutes. Use language that suits the game: "We'll need to stop after this next customer". If he gets upset, assure him you can play the game – and open up the café – again tomorrow.

In the long term…

Make it possible Set up places around your home with props for role-playing games – a toy cooker, a basket of toy fruit and veg, some dressing up items, and a doctor's kit. Take your lead from him; you don't have to join in every time he asks but do play along at least once a day.

Go with the flow Don't try to control the game or interrupt your child's flow – or he will feel you're taking over. When a young child is role-playing, he is choosing to work through the experiences that are most important to him – such as mealtimes or talking on the phone. Follow his lead and don't turn it into a lesson.

◀ SEE RELATED TOPICS ▶
Want this story: pp.76–77
What does this one do?: pp.80–81

"I want it now!"

Gratification delay is the ability to use logic to forego what you want now for the promise of a bigger reward. Children who are able to control their impulses have been found to have greater success as adults, because they make wiser and more sensible choices.

SCENARIO | **When you get a tub of ice cream out of the freezer, you tell your child it will be five minutes until it's ready to serve.**

SHE SAYS

"I want it now!"

Being told to wait will be a challenge for your child at this age. This is because delaying gratification takes executive functioning skills – or thinking and planning in the higher parts of her brain – which are still developing. Children do not start to develop this usually until between the ages of 3 and 5, and even then, it's a skill most of us continue to work on well in adulthood.

TEACHING CHILDREN HOW TO DELAY GRATIFICATION GIVES THEM A LIFE-LONG SKILL.

◄ SEE RELATED TOPICS ►

Blue cup. No, yellow cup. No, blue cup: pp.46–47
No colouring on the wall: pp.174–175

YOU MIGHT THINK

"Why does everything have to be right away? Can't she just wait?"

You might be annoyed at what feels like your child's eternal quest for instant gratification and her extreme impatience. But, while it's unrealistic to expect her to have willpower at this age, and be able to wait long for anything, you can still help her to develop patience.

WHAT SHE'S THINKING

"The ice cream's right there. Why can't I eat it now?"

To your child, ice cream is a treat that tastes so good, that the reward centres in her brain crave it as soon as she sees it. She does not yet fully understand cause and effect or have the life experience to understand it needs to soften before you can scoop it out of the tub.

HOW TO RESPOND

In the moment...

Sidetrack her Toddlers are easily distracted, so shift her attention away from the cause of her frustration – point out something else interesting, such as what the cat's up to in the garden or remind her about a new toy.

Make the time real If the ice cream needs five minutes to soften, set a timer and give her a challenge – how many Lego pieces can she can pick up before the buzzer goes off – then it's ready to eat. This gives your child a more concrete interpretation of how long she needs to wait for and gives her more control over the process.

Keep it out of sight to keep it out of mind Children find it easier to wait for something if it's out of sight. Put the ice cream somewhere your child can't see it.

In the long term...

Suggest strategies Children who sing songs to themselves or take themselves on an imaginary journey have been found to be more patient.

Talk about patience Next time your child manages to wait well, talk about the experience afterwards, for instance: "Remember how you waited so well in the queue for the fairground ride, and do you remember how much fun it was when you got your turn?"

"I'm not finished."

At this age children live in the moment and put their own needs or wants first. If they are enjoying an activity or are absorbed in a game, they can find it frustrating to stop and switch attention to something else, especially if they don't want to do it as much.

SCENARIO | **Your child is playing in the sandpit at the playground. It's time to leave to pick up your older child from school.**

HE SAYS

"I'm not finished."

YOU MIGHT THINK

"Why does he kick up such a fuss? He knows I've got to pick up his big brother."

While adults have things to do and places to be, children just want to play. It's frustrating for your child to give up his fun for something else. At this age, he can usually only focus on one activity at a time for up to 10–15 minutes, so-called "play islands". So, the best time to get him to leave his activity is at the junction of one game and another.

You know school pick-up happens at a certain time every weekday, but he's living in the moment and doesn't think about anything but his play. If he seems to drag his feet when you need to be somewhere, you may well feel frustrated.

"

DEALING WITH TRANSITIONS IS A CRUCIAL ABILITY FOR STARTING SCHOOL. TEACH YOUR CHILD WAYS HE CAN PREPARE FOR CHANGE WHILE HE IS YOUNG.

WHAT HE'S THINKING

"Why do grown-ups want to ruin my fun?"

Disrupting his game to him feels like you are deliberately ruining his entertainment. With his growing independence, he wants to be in charge of his playtime. It takes a lot of brain power and self-control for him to stop what he is doing for a reason that is important to you but not to him.

HOW TO RESPOND

In the moment...

Name your child's feelings Rather than handing out orders, show him you understand. Tell him: "I know you're having a fun time, and you're sad that we have to go now." Then, he will know you understand and won't feel the need to protest as much.

Offer specific praise When he ends his game well and comes along without a protest, tell him what's he's done right so he's more likely to do the same next time.

Make the next activity interesting If you are asking him to do something he doesn't want to do, such as sit in the back of the car to go to school, suggest singing a song or playing a guessing game in the car on the way.

In the long term...

Give him enough time to finish If you plan your departure when he's coming to the end of his game, he won't put up so much resistance. But you can also prepare him by giving lots of gentle, but firm, warnings: "One more turn making a sandcastle and then we'll go".

Become predictable Making these transitions is harder when your child is tired and hungry. Establishing a routine that revolves around him for meals, naps, and trips to the playground will help make such transitions easier for him to cope with.

▶ SEE RELATED TOPICS ▶
Just one more: pp.58–59
Let's pretend...: pp.64–65

"Please, please, please."

Now your child is able to speak, she can express her wishes in words. She is the centre of her universe, so will direct her new-found ability to ask for what she wants from you because she sees you as an all-powerful grown-up whose role it is to meet all her needs.

SCENARIO | **In the park, your child spots an ice cream cart and starts asking repeatedly for an ice cream.**

LEARNING HOW TO ASK NICELY HELPS CHILDREN AND PARENTS ENJOY THEIR TIME TOGETHER.

SHE SAYS
———
"Please, please, please."

Now your child understands cause and effect, she knows that if she keeps repeating herself, you will respond. Even if she doesn't always get what she wants, getting a reaction makes her feel powerful. Your child also repeats herself because she doesn't know how else to get what she wants.

◣ SEE RELATED TOPICS ▶
Just one more?: pp.58–59
I want it now!: pp.66–67

YOU MIGHT THINK

"Her whining makes me look like a bad parent, but a tantrum would too."

WHAT SHE'S THINKING

"I want an ice cream now. If I say it enough times, Mummy will give in."

As you're in a public place, you're likely to feel conflicted. On one hand, you recognize that her whining may turn into a tantrum, but you also feel judged by other parents who may assume you have given in to her in the past. You may also resent her for asking for treats every time you're out.

At this stage of development, children engage in "wishful thinking" and that just wanting something means they can get it. By repeating herself, she believes that she will be able to influence you into giving her what she wants.

HOW TO RESPOND

In the moment...

Show her you've heard Let your child know that you understood her request the first time.

Ask her to use her nice voice Tell your child you'll listen if she asks nicely. Then you can start to discuss whether having an ice cream is a good idea or not.

Explain why Tell her the reason for your decision. If you said no, don't make her feel greedy for asking.

Stay neutral In the past, your child's whining may have made you respond, even if you only gave her negative attention. If you get angry, her fight-or-flight instincts will kick in to deal with her frustration and a tantrum is likely to follow. Don't let whining bother you.

In the long term...

Praise self-control Notice and thank your child for controlling her impulses at other times, such as when she listens without interrupting. This doesn't mean she will always be able to do it perfectly, but she will know you are aware of her desires even when she isn't acting on them.

"Not Mummy. Want Daddy."

Now your toddler is no longer a baby and can express his desires more clearly, he is seeking more control over some aspects of his life. One of the ways he may try to do this is by choosing which parent he does different activities with.

SCENARIO | **Despite you offering to role-play pirates, your child only wants to play with Daddy; Mummy won't do.**

HE SAYS

"Not Mummy. Want Daddy."

YOU MIGHT THINK

"Does this mean he doesn't love me as much as Daddy?"

As a baby, your toddler was likely to have been mainly attached to his principal caregiver, often whoever fed him. Now he is growing older and more independent, he is realizing he is a separate person from you and is ready to develop his relationships with other family members. As a result, Daddy may become the new favourite.

After your child has shown you so much love, hearing this can be hurtful. You may wonder if you've done something wrong, or even feel jealous or resentful of your partner. However, this is a short-lived phase, so try not to take his words personally. Instead see it as sign of his growing confidence.

SEE RELATED TOPICS
Mummy, don't go!: pp.52–53
I like this stick: pp.78–79

"I just like playing with Daddy more for this kind of game."

There are many reasons why your child may ask for his other parent. If Daddy is not home as much, he may find him more exciting. But he may still want you to help him get dressed because that's what he's used to. He may also prefer Daddy for this game because studies show fathers are more likely to take part in rough-and-tumble play.

HOW TO RESPOND

In the moment...

Allow him some choice Listen to and acknowledge your child's request for his other parent. If your co-parent isn't around, tell him: "I'm right here. I can play with you until Daddy is back."

Use humour Rather than look upset, say something like: "You're right. Daddy is a good Captain Hook!" While it's important to teach that words can hurt, save this for when you are feeling less sensitive so you don't make your child feel guilty.

In the long term...

Develop your connection If you think your child may be asking for his other parent because he has more fun with him, set aside daily one-on-one time to develop fun activities you can do together too.

Be a team Children feel safest when they have a team of adult carers working together to look after them. If you can show your child you and Daddy can meet his needs equally, your roles will be more easily interchangeable and there will fewer hurt feelings when your child says he doesn't want you.

Talk to your partner Let your partner know how you feel so resentment doesn't build up between you. Avoid making critical comments in front of your child and set aside more time together as a family.

Sleep difficulties

All parents know that children are happier and better behaved when they are well rested. However that doesn't mean that children welcome going to bed – or that they will stay in bed throughout the night.

Generally, children tend to have two main types of sleep problem – not wanting to go to bed in the first place and then waking up during the night.

In the first instance, some children don't want to go to sleep because being alone in the dark can bring on feelings of separation anxiety. Some children's minds are active and they can find it hard to transition to a more relaxed state of mind. Children have more periods of light sleep than adults and have yet to learn that when they stir, it is not always time to wake up, and so need to learn to settle themselves back down to sleep.

Getting a child into a sleep routine is one of the hardest parenting challenges. But when you achieve it, it can make one of the most positive differences to family life. See your role as helping your child develop a healthy attitude to sleep and enjoy time in her bed.

1
Find out the problem
Count how many hours your child sleeps in a week. Think about why your child does not want to go bed. Is she craving time with you? Napping too much? Address any issues first.

4
Make bedtime special
Never threaten to send your child to bed as a punishment. Portray bedtime as a special time to snuggle up with a book before she gets the rest she needs to grow well, learn, and have lots of energy.

7
Don't rush it
To help soothe your child's active brain and help her make the transition, allow up to an hour from starting bath-time to lights out.

9
Keep it low key
After lights out, help meet any need for a drink, a toilet visit, or a quick hug for reassurance, but try to engage as little as possible so your child is not rewarded with your attention.

GOOD PRACTICE
10 key principles

2
Create a plan
Consistency is key, so work out a plan that you and your family can stick to. Decide on one change at a time – such as getting your child to bed without a row or getting her to stay in bed all night. Changes can take up to two weeks.

3
Present a united front
Disagreements over how and when to get children into bed can cause tension between partners who lose out on precious adult time. If your child gets mixed messages, she may try to play you off against one other.

5
Tell your child what they are doing right
Notice and describe everything your child does right as she gets ready for bed, from getting out of the bath without a fuss, to putting on her pyjamas without being asked.

6
Create sleep cues
Night-time routines are full of signals associated with falling asleep. As adults, we take these cues for granted – getting undressed, brushing teeth, and reading a book in bed. Create these cues for your child by doing the steps in the same order every night.

8
Get a night-light
Young children can feel as if the darkness hides all the familiar objects in their bedroom. A dim nightlight can show them nothing has changed and doesn't interrupt their sleep.

10
Help her see sleep as a positive
Without adult help, children don't understand the link between getting enough sleep and feeling grumpy the next day. As she gets older, point this out as well as how hard it is to get up when she doesn't get enough sleep.

TAILORED ADVICE
Age by age

2–3
YEAR-OLDS

Snooze, don't lose
Your child needs about 12–13 hours of sleep at this stage. So make sure they get to bed at the right time.

Rewarding behaviour
Use star charts and an incentive for reaching one goal at a time – for example, for staying in bed all night.

4–5
YEAR-OLDS

Scrap the nap
By now your child may need a bit less sleep, so you may want to give up daytime naps now.

Gradual changes
If it's getting harder to get your child up for school in the mornings, bring lights-out forward by 15 minutes a week until you reach your goal bedtime.

6–7
YEAR-OLDS

Bedtime creep
Homework can edge bedtimes later now. Ask your child's teacher how much time homework should take and help her child stick to it.

Any worries?
Some children find it harder to sleep at this age due to friendship or school worries. Ask your child to write down any concerns before bed so she can process and talk through them with you.

"Want this story."

Sharing books helps children learn to speak, interact, improve their attention span, and read sooner themselves. When part of a routine, story time helps to signal that it's time for sleep. Such undivided attention will make your child feel safe, special, and connected to you.

SCENARIO | **Your child wants you to read that story – again – at bedtime.**

HE SAYS

"Want this story."

YOU MIGHT THINK

"I've read this book 100 times. It's so repetitive."

Sharing a story is a calm and relaxing way for your child to wind down. Beyond giving him a cue to sleep, story time comes with many benefits: children who are read to frequently at ages 2 or 3 do better academically once they start school.

You probably know many books by heart, since your child will lean towards favourites and will want to hear them again and again. While the lack of variety can be frustrating for you, letting him choose allows him to feel important and direct the fun of story time.

READING STORIES IS A PRECIOUS OPPORTUNITY TO BOND, RELAX, HAVE FUN, AND HELP YOUR CHILD LEARN ALL AT THE SAME TIME.

WHAT HE'S THINKING

"Can we read it again? It makes me feel so good."

Cuddling up around a book makes your child feel secure. Rereading the same story helps your child recognize the shape of the words on the page, an essential precursor for reading. It is also a chance to practise his new vocabulary, improve his memory, and develop his emotional understanding of people – a skill he needs to build friendships.

HOW TO RESPOND

In the moment...

Give your child your full attention Let your child relax knowing this is time for the two of you and you are his priority now. Put phones out of sight.

Answer any questions Sometimes continuous interruptions are frustrating for adults. But your child's questions are key to help him interact with the story and for stretching his imagination. Talk about what he thinks will happen next and the characters' feelings.

Use lots of expression Bring stories to life by giving characters different voices to match their personalities. Trying out various voices and volumes can help your child understand the meaning of new words. The more he enjoys the story, the more he is likely to learn from it.

In the long term...

Agree your books upfront If your child often asks you to read half his bookshelf, suggest he chooses three every night at the start of story time and stick to those.

Make it a ritual Read him at least one book at bedtime as well as stories during the day, if that's possible. They don't have to be long. Even if you are tired, it's important for him to have a peaceful, calm, one-on-one time with you in the evenings, which makes him feel secure.

SEE RELATED TOPICS
Let's pretend...: pp.64–65
Carving out quality time: pp.84–85

"I like this stick."

When you pushed your child in the pram or buggy, you knew roughly how long it would take to get from A to B. But now your child is walking by herself, it feels like it can take ages to get anywhere because she is fascinated by so much of what she sees.

SCENARIO | **On the way to playgroup, your child insists on stopping to inspect yet another interesting stick.**

THIS IS A UNIQUE TIME OF EXPLORATION FOR YOUR CHILD. ADAPT YOUR PACE TO FIT IN WITH HERS.

SHE SAYS

"I like this stick."

This is the first time your child's been able to fully explore the outside world independently, so she only has to walk a few steps before she finds something new to fascinate her. She's curious about the texture, colour, and weight of her discoveries. It's as if she's seeing the world for the first time.

SEE RELATED TOPICS

I'm not finished: pp.68–69
What does this one do?: pp.80–81

YOU MIGHT THINK

"Not another stick! We're going to be late now."

WHAT SHE'S THINKING

"This stick is interesting. Why do I have to hurry?"

If you need to be somewhere at a specific time, it's easy to get frustrated when the journey progresses slowly. You may feel as if your child's ignoring your request to hurry up, but her intense focus and the fact that she can only think about one thing at a time mean she finds it hard to hear you.

Your child is building connections between her brain cells at a speed of 1,000 a second. She's programmed to make the most of this rapid cognitive development stage by noticing everything. She is living "in the moment" and it takes a lot of brain power to switch from her agenda to yours.

HOW TO RESPOND

In the moment...

Get down to her level Instead of pressing your child to hurry up, crouch down to let her show you what she's found. When you need to get going, give her a minute's notice to help her switch focus back to moving on.

Relish the journey To enjoy these walks more, try mindful walking, which has been found to have the bonus of lifting your mood. So, try walking slowly, looking around, and paying attention to everything. Adopting this approach on some walks will help you both feel happier.

In the long term...

Build in buffer time The more time pressure you put on yourself to get to places, the more difficult it will be to step into your child's world. Children learn best when they are not hurried and follow their own interests.

Meet her needs Sometimes resisting your request is a way for your child to gain some control and attention. Give her one-on-one time at other times so she doesn't feel the need to dig her heels in when you're out.

Take her outside more The outdoors is the best place for young children to practise physical skills. Away from the constraints of indoors, it allows your child freedom to run and jump, feel adventurous, and develop her senses.

"What does this one do?"

Children are natural explorers. They are born with the innate drive to discover more about the world and how it works. The more inquisitive a child is, the more he learns. While parents don't instil this curiosity, they can encourage it, with life-long benefits.

SCENARIO | **After seeing you take some photos, your child wants to play with your camera to learn how it works.**

HE SAYS

"What does this one do?"

YOU MIGHT THINK

"I wish he'd stop fiddling with everything. He's going to lose my settings."

Children's brains are wired for curiosity. As your child's higher brain develops, he starts to seek logical answers to explain how the world works. This curiosity not only helps build up his frontal lobes but also releases dopamine, a brain chemical that makes him feel good and want to explore more.

Because your child is always twiddling knobs and pushing buttons, you may feel you can't take your eyes off him for a second. However, it's important that you welcome his curiosity, rather than get annoyed by it, so he feels safe and encouraged in his quest for answers.

SEE RELATED TOPICS
Want your phone: pp.56–57
When is tomorrow?: pp.86–87

YOUR ENCOURAGEMENT IS A KEY FACTOR IN KEEPING THE DRIVE TO LEARN STRONG.

WHAT HE'S THINKING

"This makes a great noise. And I want to see how this bit works."

Your child is fascinated by cause and effect – he loves the fact that he can press a button to make something happen - just like a jack-in-the box. This gives him a sense of control over his world and helps him learn how to anticipate events.

HOW TO RESPOND

In the moment...

Describe what the buttons do By explaining what each button does in simple words, your child can combine his enquiring brain and linguistic skills to start to form a basic understanding of the world, which he can build on to find out more.

Ask him questions Take time to demonstrate what the camera does, but ask him questions, too, to help him draw on higher-level thinking and embed his learning. Make it a two-way process.

Work on the answer together Often you won't know the answers either. But in order to encourage him to keep asking questions say: "Good question. Let's find out" when you are not sure.

In the long term...

Model curiosity Show your child how to engage in life by exploring and asking questions about the world around him.

Be patient Be prepared to answer the same question more than once. While curiosity is important throughout life, studies have found that, by the age of the 7, children ask substantially fewer question if they are not encouraged. If your child feels discouraged from asking questions, he will stop.

"One for you, one for me."

Learning to share is an important skill, which has to be taught to all children. It's good to role model sharing as much as possible, so children will do the same with their peers. Being able to share is a key factor in helping them make and keep friends.

SCENARIO | Your child is making a show of sharing out her biscuits – even though you don't really want any.

SHE SAYS

"One for you, one for me."

YOU MIGHT THINK

"I really don't want a well-handled biscuit. I'll just say no."

As your child gained more control over her body, first she learned she had the ability to grab things and wanted to keep everything to herself. Now, she's reaching a new milestone – developing the empathy to realize that others have wants, too, while also mastering her impulses to hog it all.

All parents want their children to be good sharers, because they want them to be seen as kind and be liked by others. But you may have to wait until your child is about 3 before she understands she makes others happy by sharing. Until that time, encourage and reinforce her sharing offers.

SEE RELATED TOPICS
That's mine!: pp.36–37
Let's pretend…: pp.64–65

SHARING HAS TO BE TAUGHT, SO SHOW YOUR CHILD HOW TO DO IT. IT IS A CENTRAL SKILL FOR FRIENDSHIPS.

WHAT SHE'S THINKING

"I like this rule. It makes me feel good and makes Mummy happy."

Children love to repeat things they enjoy, and your child is no exception. The more she repeats such rituals with you, the more she's learning how to share – an important skill for her future.

HOW TO RESPOND

In the moment...

(1)

Smile and take the biscuit Reinforce the message that sharing is good, by encouraging sharing with your child and others as much as you can.

(2)

Thank her Let her know you're grateful for her fairness and generosity; you can always say you're saving your biscuit for later.

In the long term...

Describe what she's doing right Use descriptive praise to tell your child when she has shared well. For example, "Did you see how Laura smiled when you gave her a biscuit? She really liked it when you did that."

Explain what sharing means Help her see when sharing means it's gone forever (as with food) and when she'll get it back later (as with lending a toy).

Play sharing games Board games and games that involve turn-taking offer ways to practise sharing.

Carving out quality time

However busy life gets, it's important to set aside a period every day to give your child undivided love and attention. Such regular one-on-one times are likely to be the most special moments for both of you.

In children's eyes, the word "love" really does equate to "time" – it may sound corny, but it's true. Even if you're working hard to provide for them, children can process your busy-ness as rejection, so carving out precious time to be with them is really worthwhile.

While you can't create more hours in the day, you can prioritize the setting aside of some special time in what you do have. Be reassured that all your efforts will be rewarded. Such together times are when your child feels most close to you – and some of your best memories are made.

It's good to know, too, that a lot of attention-seeking behaviour, jealousy, and whining can be headed off when your child knows there's always going to be a period in the day when he feels like he's the most important person in the world to you.

Set aside 10–15 minutes
Aim for short chunks daily with each child and be consistent. You will enjoy these times and soon start to reap the behavioural benefits.

Make the most of holidays
As well as recharging batteries, holidays are key bonding times. Really connect with your child by creating opportunities for "attachment play", where you sit or stand opposite your child, which relays "I love being with you".

Find the best time of day
Whether you choose to get up a bit earlier and start your day sitting on your child's bed, stroking his hair, and chatting about the day ahead or have some extra quiet time before bedtime at the end of the day is up to you. Find what works best for you and your child.

GOOD PRACTICE
8 key principles

2
Label it
It's key that your child understands that you have set aside this time to be with him. At the start, tell him it's your "special time" together.

3

Focus on the freebies
Spend time with your child on activities that don't cost money. There's so much you can do – playing card games, cooking, taking family walks or bike rides, and walking the dog – to show that just being together is enough.

5
Maximize every opportunity
Whenever you are with just one child, running errands or in the car, for example, be aware that this time can easily become meaningful if you tune into their moods and interests – ask him what he'd like to talk about.

7
Have fun together
Fun activities release feel-good neurochemicals and contribute to a positive self-identity.

8
Turn off the tech
Always put away your phone. Try to clear your mind of other things, so you can stay present with your child.

SETTING ASIDE EVEN A SHORT AMOUNT OF 'SPECIAL TIME' DAILY CAN GO A LONG WAY TOWARDS IMPROVING YOUR BOND.

TAILORED ADVICE
Age by age

2–3
YEAR-OLDS

Cuddles please
Children are still reliant on touch to help them feel close and comforted.

Whatever you say
When possible, give your child the choice of what to do together. It sends the message: "I don't mind what we do. This is about being with you."

4–5
YEAR-OLDS

A little helper
Now your child is a little older, ask them to help you cook dinner or fix things around the house.

All ears
When your child tells you about school, don't try to teach or advise. Just listening and reflecting back what he says is often enough. The best question is often: "Tell me why".

6–7
YEAR-OLDS

Staggered bedtimes
If you have a younger child, once a week let your older child stay up half an hour past his usual bedtime so you can do something as just the two of you.

Taxi time
Often older children find it easier to talk about things that are bothering them if they don't have to make eye contact – travelling in the car is one such opportunity.

"When is tomorrow?"

Adults think a lot about time, whether it's minutes and hours, or yesterday, today, and tomorrow. Young children only understand what they can touch or feel; time is an abstract concept and they need help to understand when things are going to happen.

SCENARIO | **Your child knows her grandparents are visiting tomorrow, but she keeps asking where they are.**

SHE SAYS

"When is tomorrow?"

> **YOUNG CHILDREN ARE NOT BEING UNREASONABLE WHEN THEY SHOW IMPATIENCE. THEY CANNOT YET SEE HOW TIME PASSES.**

Your child lives mainly in the moment. Her concept of the passage of time is based on knowing that things happen regularly — getting up, eating meals, and going to bed. By hearing you link such happenings to words, she will start to understand what you mean when you say "later" or "before". But "tomorrow" is still too far away for her to imagine.

◄ **SEE RELATED TOPICS** ►

Want your phone: pp.56–57
I want it now: pp.66–67

YOU MIGHT THINK

"I've told her so many times they aren't coming until tomorrow. Why is she so impatient?"

WHAT SHE'S THINKING

"I want my grandparents to come now. It feels like forever."

Adult lives are ruled by times and deadlines, so it's easy to forget that these mean nothing to a young child. It's hard to fight feelings of exasperation when your child asks repeatedly when the visitors are arriving. But know that she can't comprehend "tomorrow" and remain calm.

Her brain's higher functions for looking into the future are not yet developed. In her mind, your child is so excited about seeing Grandma and Grandpa that she thinks it should happen now. Her lack of practice in delaying gratification also makes her impatient.

HOW TO RESPOND

In the moment...

Chunk it up Tell her you understand she wants to see Grandma and Grandpa now, but if she has dinner, then a bath, a story, and goes to bed, the time will add up and they will be here after she's finished her breakfast tomorrow.

Distract her Offer her activities and distractions, so that she won't focus entirely on her grandparents' arrival.

In the long term...

Give her a routine Children understand how time passes more clearly if they have a routine – they can use the benchmarks in their day to measure the passing of time.

Link activities to times Throughout the day, use different time words to help her understand when things happen. Talk about putting her coat on "before" going outside or eating pudding "after" her main course.

Track passing time Use visual tools to help your child comprehend time. For example, you could stick a photo of Grandma and Grandpa on the calendar on the day of their visit and cross off each day as it passes, so she can see their arrival get closer.

your
4 — 5
YEAR-OLD

"I want a cuddle."

At this age, your child is programmed to be attached and stay close to the person he spends the most time with and who makes him feel the most safe. Even when children start to strike out on their own, they still need the security of an adult and a comforting cuddle.

SCENARIO | Your child won't leave your arms to join in a friend's birthday party.

HE SAYS

"I want a cuddle."

Despite your child knowing most of the children at this party, when you arrive the novelty and noise may be overwhelming. He may need reassurance and security from you. He may be thinking: "Help, this is new and scary to me."

"

INTRODUCE HIM TO OTHERS FROM THE SAFETY OF YOUR ARMS, SO HE CAN OBSERVE HIS SURROUNDINGS AND GET USED TO THEM FIRST.

YOU MIGHT THINK

"He normally can't wait to go off and explore. Why is he being so clingy today?"

Acknowledge that this behaviour, though surprising, is a sign that he trusts you to comfort him – your child can signal that he still wants you to keep him safe in this unfamiliar place. Ask yourself if he's ready to be this independent. Enjoy the cuddles while he plucks up the courage to join in.

WHAT HE'S THINKING

"Mum don't let go. I want to feel a bit braver before I join in."

Research has found that 10 to 20 per cent of children come into the world wired with slightly more vigilant nervous systems, which makes them more cautious in new situations. It doesn't mean your child won't make friends. He just needs you a little longer as his secure base.

HOW TO RESPOND

In the moment...

Don't force him to join in Do cuddle and keep him close. And avoid saying he's a big boy now and he must run along and play. Give him time to adjust to the situation.

Get him noticing what's going on Keep him focused outwards by pointing out what's going on, whether it's the birthday cake on the table or a friendly party game in progress. Something will catch his eye that will make it hard for him to resist joining in.

Don't label him as "shy" Acknowledge his feelings – that he's unsure about the party because it is crowded – but avoid referring to him as shy or he will feel permanently branded as such. Cuddle him without question or judgment.

Praise his bravery When he does start to look around and show an interest in joining in, give him targeted praise. Tell him you know it's tricky but he's done really well and is brave to join in.

In the long term...

Practise social situations Take your child with you when you go out so he gets practice meeting others in smaller groups and quieter places. Your child needs to be in social situations to learn how to be social. Let him see you being outgoing and happy to meet people, too, at parties or at school and neighbourhood events.

SEE RELATED TOPICS

Shyness: pp.62–63
I want my dummy: pp.94–95

"Look what I've done!"

Your 4- or 5-year-old will be very clear about wanting you to take notice of her and what she does. We all have a fundamental psychological need for recognition, but children especially need lots of positive attention for healthy cognitive and emotional development.

SCENARIO | **Your child has just finished her favourite puzzle.**

SHE SAYS

"Look what I've done!"

YOU MIGHT THINK

"I have so much to do. Why does she want me to see that again?"

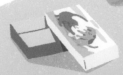

She is desperate for you to come over and look at it immediately. We are programmed from birth to need recognition and be acknowledged by others. This is one of the key building blocks of self-worth.

Whether or not your child has achieved something new is irrelevant – she can't help but crave your recognition. Interruptions can be irksome but if you show you're angry or irritated, then she might seek attention instead by misbehaving. Your loving attention is what's needed now.

YOUR ATTENTION, PRAISE, AND UNCONDITIONAL LOVE ARE THE BIGGEST INFLUENCES ON YOUR CHILD.

WHAT SHE'S THINKING

"Please don't ignore me, your approval is really important!"

Not only does your child want your attention, but she also needs your social approval. Children have a built-in radar to detect praise that doesn't sound meant or intended. She'll process any lack of sincerity or distraction (being glued to your phone, for instance) as rejection.

SEE RELATED TOPICS
You're always too busy: pp.128–129
You promised: pp.168–169

HOW TO RESPOND

In the moment...

Stop what you're doing (if it's safe to do so) And give your child your undivided attention – if only for a few moments. Even a short burst of positive attention will satisfy her hunger for recognition and make her feel secure and valued. If you can't stop immediately, tell her "I'll come as soon as I've..." and then keep your word. You may want to suggest something she can do while she's waiting for you to finish.

Notice what she's done right Instead of just reeling off another "Well done," take a moment to notice what she's done and refer to something specific: "I really like the colours in that jigsaw" or "What a fun picture".

Show unsolicited approval from time to time Offer encouraging words even when she isn't asking for it directly – for example, if you notice her playing well or being cooperative. Frequent bursts of attention and comments during the day will help build her confidence and self-belief as well as discover exactly what sort of behaviour you want to see.

In the long term...

Avoid delaying tactics "I'm busy; wait a minute." Chances are a minute will turn into several minutes, and the opportunity may pass. Not stopping at that moment means you're repeatedly denying her calls for attention – such an approach can knock her confidence and self-belief.

Make it work for you You don't always have to sit down and play to give your child positive attention and praise. It's your attention and recognition she wants; she will also love copying you and doing whatever it is you're doing. Enjoy such quality moments.

"I want my dummy."

Sucking has a powerfully calming effect, which is why many parents give their babies dummies to help them soothe themselves. But as they grow older, children can find letting go of this habit hard without lots of encouragement.

SCENARIO | **Your child is ready to start school. But he still insists on having his dummy for most of the day.**

HE SAYS

"I want my dummy."

You may well have started using a dummy as a way to help your baby or young child relax and go to sleep, but over time it has become a comfort for him in the daytime, too. He may feel he needs his dummy to relax, but he just needs to learn other ways of regulating emotions.

" "

YOUR CHILD'S DUMMY IS OUTLIVING ITS PURPOSE AND, WITH YOUR HELP, YOUR CHILD IS READY TO FIND NEW WAYS TO SOOTHE HIMSELF.

YOU MIGHT THINK

"He's far too old to still have a dummy. It makes him look like a baby."

Your child's dummy is a transitional object – something that soothes him when you are not there. Now he's 4 you may feel embarrassed that he still uses it and worry other parents see you as lazy for allowing him to become dependent on it, let alone how it might impact his teeth and his speech.

SEE RELATED TOPICS
I want a cuddle: pp.90–91
I've lost teddy: pp.126–127

WHAT HE'S THINKING

"My dummy makes me feel safe. I can't feel better without it."

Your child's brain has created an association between sucking on the dummy and feeling calm – it's become a habit. He may be upset at first, but if he is praised for going without his dummy for ever-longer periods (with distractions), the habit loop will be broken.

HOW TO RESPOND

In the moment...

①

Talk to your child Explain how he is now big and brave enough not to need a dummy any more. While some children will need to be weaned off their habit, others may decide to give theirs up because it looks babyish.

②

Offer alternatives Before you take away the dummy, show your child ways to feel calm and safe – singing to himself, holding a cuddly toy close, or talking to you. If he is very resistant, take small steps, rewarding and recognizing him for every hour he manages to go without it and offer him plenty of games to distract him.

In the long term...

Wean him off Agree some parameters with him for how long he can use it each day and where; then gradually tweak these to reduce his use further. For example, you may say he can only use it upstairs and then, later, only in bed. Put it away – out of sight is really out of mind.

Give a reward Many children respond to the positive rewards of a star chart. Give him some notice and say at the end of the period, he can collect all his dummies together and put them in a box to be recycled overnight. Then he will have reward waiting for him the next morning.

Select the time carefully Choose a stress-free period when you can be around to offer comfort and distraction – a holiday or period of time off work is ideal. Expect it to take up to two weeks for him to stop asking for it.

"Are you sad, Mummy?"

As a parent, you're used to responding when your child cries in distress or because she has hurt herself, but you may be surprised the first time she tries to comfort you when you're sad. Discussing your emotions at times with your child can help her develop emotional intelligence.

SCENARIO | After a stressful day, your child finds you in tears.

SHE SAYS

"Are you sad, Mummy?"

Previously only able to see the world from her point of view, your child is now old enough to understand that you also have emotions that are influenced by external events, so she knows something must have happened to make you cry.

YOU MIGHT THINK

"I don't want my child to see me like this. Maybe I shouldn't cry in front of her?"

Your child tends to see you as an all-powerful "superhero" figure, so you may be embarrassed to show your vulnerable side. However, children learn their emotional understanding from their main carers, so the fact that your child is able to show you her understanding is a testament to the empathetic parenting she has received from you.

"TELL YOUR CHILD THAT CRYING CAN HELP OUR SADNESS TO COME OUT AND HELPS US TO FEEL BETTER AFTERWARDS.

WHAT SHE'S THINKING

"Why is Mummy so sad? Is it something I've done?"

For any child, it can be scary to see their parent, who is their emotional rock, feeling overwhelmed. Since children also put themselves at the centre of every situation, your child may think you're crying because of something she has done.

HOW TO RESPOND

In the moment...

Be open Crying is a normal, natural reaction to emotional or physical pain. Don't be ashamed of crying in front of your child, or tell her that crying is "babyish".

Talk through your feelings Without going into too much detail, explain the core reasons you are sad using "I feel" statements so that she learns to take responsibility for her feelings, too. For example, "I feel sad today because I had an argument with my friend. But I am sure I'll feel a lot better after we've played a game."

Reassure her Most of all, children want to know that they are safe and will always be looked after and loved. Give your child lots of smiles and hugs after you've cried. Make it clear that you were not shedding tears because of anything she has said or done.

In the long term...

Foster emotional intelligence Help your child develop emotional intelligence by showing her how you name your feelings, such as sadness and frustration. And when times are tough, make the most of the support from adults around you. Your child will then see that talking to peers is a positive step towards feeling better.

Talk about your positive emotions too No emotion is bad, but we tend to pay more attention to the negative ones. Talk to your child about times when you feel happy too. This will help her to notice and appreciate different emotions and to see that life contains a mix of feelings.

SEE RELATED TOPICS
I want a cuddle: pp.90–91
They say I'm a cry baby: pp.138–139

"I'm going to explode."

Anger is a secondary emotion, which takes time to learn how to control. It is often triggered by feelings of frustration, fear, or sadness. Some children need more help to be able to control their tempers after they suffer disappointments or frustrations.

SCENARIO | **Your child loses his temper after waiting to go on a swing when another child takes it as it becomes free.**

HE SAYS

"I'm going to explode."

YOU MIGHT THINK

"Why does he always get in such a strop? It's just a turn on a swing."

Every parent hopes their child's tantrums will fade as they get older and learn to regulate their emotions when their hopes or expectations are not met. But, some children, born with more "wired" temperaments, need more assistance from grown-ups to notice their negative feelings, work out how to deal with them, and modify their behaviour.

If your child often loses his temper, you may be on tenterhooks for the next outburst. You might also be embarrassed as you fear others will think your child should have grown out of this tantrum-style behaviour, or worry that his temper will put other children off wanting to be his friends.

HELP YOUR CHILD TO RECOGNIZE THE TRIGGERS THAT IGNITE HIS ANGER AND HOW TO DEAL WITH THEM BEFORE THEY SEND HIM INTO A TEMPER.

WHAT HE'S THINKING

"It's not fair the other child got my turn. I feel so cross – like a volcano."

Your child already knows he should not overreact, but he is at the mercy of his feelings and doesn't know how to put the brakes on them. The alarm system in his lower brain is hair-trigger sensitive. So, when stress hormones flood his body, he loses his temper before rational thinking kicks in. What he wants is to feel safe and back in control.

SEE RELATED TOPICS
You have to: pp.150–151
It feels nice: pp.162–163

HOW TO RESPOND

In the moment...

Handle it like a tantrum The first thing to do is help him calm down from his hyper-aroused state. Move him somewhere quiet, where others are not watching him, so he can regain control of his higher thinking.

Keep calm Getting angry with your child for being angry is like throwing petrol on a fire. Maintain eye contact and use short simple sentences such as "It's going to be OK" or "big breaths". Offer a cuddle. Tell him that there's nothing wrong with anger, but he needs to control what he does with it.

In the long term...

Give him practice Try making a game of trying different challenging situations, such as letting others go before him in a queue or losing a game, and ask him to try different ways of handling his reaction. Talk about how such minor irritations are never the end of the world.

Keep your child's tank full Make sure your child gets plenty of sleep and regular healthy meals and exercise. Without them, he will be already putting his system under stress, and he will be more easily triggered.

Help him understand his feelings Get him to notice how his body tenses up when he starts to become angry and to spot the signs that he needs to step away from the situation. Help him visualize his anger as a volcano or firework about to go off. By seeing anger as something outside himself, he will find it easier to talk about.

"I'm just going to do it."

All children are naturally impulsive: it takes time and practice to control their actions and not do the first thing that comes into their heads. Be patient while your child learns to apply her "mental brakes" before doing something she knows she shouldn't.

SCENARIO | **You told your child not to start painting until her apron is on, but she starts anyway and gets paint on her clothes.**

SHE SAYS

"I'm just going to do it."

YOU MIGHT THINK

"When I tell her not to do something, why can't she just do as she's told?"

Children learn self-control with guidance from you and plenty of practice. She is also learning that her behaviour has consequences. However, learning impulse-control can be a slow process. Although she is getting better, she can't apply it all the time, especially when she's excited.

When you expressly tell a child not to do something, it can be frustrating when she seems to deliberately defy you. You may also feel impatient that she cannot yet follow clear rules or believe she should know better.

CHILDREN ARE NATURALLY IMPULSIVE. HELP THEM TO MAINTAIN THEIR NATURAL CURIOSITY WHILE LEARNING TO LIVE BY RULES.

WHAT SHE'S THINKING

"I'm so excited about painting, I can't wait to get started even though Mummy told me not to."

At this age, the thinking-planning part of your child's brain is maturing all the time. This is the "chairperson" in her mind, which has the final say in whether to do something or not. Sometimes, the emotional or physical urge to do something can be so great that it overrules logic or reason, but over time, the "chairperson" will gain more control.

SEE RELATED TOPICS
Do it myself: pp.38–39
Look what I've done!: pp.92–93

HOW TO RESPOND

In the moment...

Give consequences Set boundaries and explain your reasons. Rather than be angry when she breaks these, which will send her into a fight-or-flight response where she'll find it harder to process what you're saying, give her immediate and direct consequences so she learns cause and effect. For example: "You didn't wait for your apron, so now you'll have to wait longer to start while you change your top."

Repeat the instruction If your child looks distracted and as if she's not listening, check she has processed what you have asked her to do by saying: "Please explain to me what I just told you."

In the long term...

Be patient Parents can have unrealistic expectations of their child's ability to control their impulses. Rather than get frustrated, or compare her with children who you think are better behaved, remember that some children simply have more impulsive natures. Accept that she may need more time and practice to master these feelings.

Talk about your own impulse control Show her how you exercise self-control over your decisions and don't rush to the do the first thing you feel like doing. For example, tell her: "I'd really like to read a book now, but first I'm going to tidy the room so it's nice to sit in."

Explain how her brain works Help her feel in control of her impulses by giving her a very simple explanation of how her brain works. Tell her that she has a "downstairs brain" that makes her want to do everything she wants right away, and an "upstairs brain" that helps her make more sensible decisions. If she doesn't rush, she can make use of her "upstairs brain".

"That's so funny!"

Laughing with your child is one of the best ways to feel closer, as well as brighten up family life. A good sense of humour can also make your child happier, more optimistic, and more resilient in the face of the ups and downs of childhood, as well as boost self-esteem.

SCENARIO | Even while you're doing household chores, your child loves telling you jokes and making you laugh.

HE SAYS

"That's so funny!"

Telling jokes is an important milestone. Having learned what's normal, your child finds jokes funny because they portray an absurd world in which characters do or say unexpected things. Encouraging your child's humour strengthens the bond between you. A sense of humour will also help him make and keep friends as he gets older.

> "LAUGHTER BENEFITS CHILDREN'S WELLBEING. HUMOUR CAN BE TAUGHT THROUGH PLAYFUL PARENTING."

SEE RELATED TOPICS
I love being with you: pp.108–109
When I was little…: pp.114–115

WHAT HE'S THINKING

"It makes me feel good when I make Daddy laugh."

There will be times when you may tire of your child's more repetitive jokes. But being able to play with incongruous ideas – such as a cow knocking on a door or a chicken crossing the road – are novel for him. Enjoy the fact that his joke-telling shows he loves interacting with you.

Humour shows your child is using the left side of his brain to process language and the right to work out what's unusual about a jokey situation, which makes it humorous. He is also learning to sequence events, so jokes are satisfying when they have a clear punch-line.

HOW TO RESPOND

In the moment...

Play along Be playful around your child and make light of small disasters, such as a juice spill, so you enjoy your time together more. Children laugh most when there are others to play with, so make time for playful interaction.

Mirror your child's humour Be aware of what your child finds funny so you can reflect it back. If you try humour on him that is too sophisticated, such as irony, which he will not yet understand, he will be confused.

In the long term...

Gloss over toilet humour At this age, many children find toilet jokes hilarious. But showing disgust or embarrassment when your child jokes about this in front of others may just reinforce the idea that this humour is taboo – making it even funnier.

Track his development Children's humour progresses from peek-a-boo to slapstick and nonsense words through to wordplay by the age of 7. What your child finds funny also tells you how his mind is developing.

Practise being funny Laughter activates reward pathways in the brain, boosts immunity, and reduces stress. So, keep humour at the heart of family life.

"Can Mr Giraffe sit down, too?"

Most young children play pretend games and talk to their dolls or toy animals as if they were real. Almost 40 per cent take such play further and create an invisible friend. Your child is more likely to do this if she's an only child or if there's a big age gap with older siblings.

SCENARIO | Your child insists on setting a place at the table at every meal for her imaginary friend.

SHE SAYS

"Can Mr Giraffe sit down, too?"

YOU MIGHT THINK

"Is this OK? Is it normal to have an imaginary friend?"

In trying to find areas of life where she can exert power, your child may think it's fun to have made-up friends because she can play what she likes and she can decide what happens next.

You may worry that inventing an imaginary friend means your child is lonely, but it's perfectly normal. Such a friend (whether invisible or a personified object such as Mr Giraffe) gives her a chance to stretch her imagination, talk about feelings, work through worries, and exert control.

SEE RELATED TOPICS
I've lost teddy: pp.126–127
I didn't do it: pp.142–143

"I love playing with him. And I can blame him for the naughty things I do."

 Your child knows her friend exists only in her mind. But she'd like to include him as much as possible in the real world. And if that means as an accomplice to things she's not supposed to do, that'll do just fine.

HOW TO RESPOND

In the moment...

(1)

Play along Never tell your child off for making up her friend, but be clear you know he is fictitious. Ask her to set up Mr Giraffe's dinner place in her room, for instance. This lets her know you are aware how vital he is, but helps to draw a line between real and imaginary lives.

(2)

Don't let him become a scapegoat If your child blames Mr Giraffe for things she knows are naughty or says he told her to do them, it may be a sign you are disciplining her too harshly – maybe she is scared to take responsibility. Try to rethink and be more understanding.

In the long term...

Help her develop real friendships As well as having Mr Giraffe as a playmate, set up play dates so she can spend time with real peers, with all the negotiation, compromise, and fun that involves.

Listen in By paying attention to your child's conversations with her imaginary playmate you can get a sense of what's going on in her mind. Children can use imaginary friends to fulfil unmet needs or wishes they find hard to express to adults.

Remember it's a phase Most imaginary friends fall out of favour after the age of 7 or 8 when pretend play also subsides. Despite the intensity of such relationships, many kids forget about their friend as they get older.

Moving home

To small children, home is their entire world, so the sight of it being dismantled in front of them can be overwhelming. By seeing the transition through your child's eyes, there's a lot you can do to help him settle sooner.

Parents are often told that moving is one of life's most stressful experiences. And while some children will view it as a huge adventure – depending on age, temperament, and circumstances – others will view leaving their old home as a loss of all they have come to know.

Unless you explain it, children may also be confused by what's happening. For example, they may not realize that they can take all their belongings with them, or that their pets can come too. They may also be anxious to see the familiar objects they have grown up with – including their toys – disappear into huge boxes. If you're relocating, older children in particular will worry about starting a new school and finding new friends. Taking a little time to help your child understand what to expect can make the transition smoother for the whole family.

" "

MAKE IT CLEAR THAT A HOME IS NOT ABOUT THE BUILDING, BUT THE LOVE THAT HAPPENS INSIDE.

1
Prepare for change
Take your child on a tour of their new home, and make it clear the move is permanent. Explain the process so they understand they are switching from living in one place to another, not going on holiday.

4
Let them make future plans
To help your child feel more comfortable in their new home, let them make as many safe choices as possible about how to make it cosy, whether it's choosing the colour of their new bedroom, or thinking of a funny name for their new place to live.

6

Get childcare on moving day
Moving is stressful for everyone, so ask a close friend or relative to take your child out for the day once you've arrived. Otherwise, they may feel left out or in the way because you're busy.

Age by age

2–3
YEAR-OLDS

The right time
Leave explanations as late as you can, but before the packing starts, so they're not living with the uncertainty for too long.

Avoiding overload
Hold off other stressful transitions, such as toilet training, until your child has settled. Be understanding if they regress, for example, by wanting a bottle.

4–5
YEAR-OLDS

Acting it out
Help your child understand the transition by role-playing with toy lorries, doll's houses, or shoe boxes to represent your old and new homes.

Story time subjects
There are many storybooks written for children about moving, which will help them understand the process.

6–7
YEAR-OLDS

Same but different
If your child has to move school, take them on a tour beforehand. Emphasize that they will be learning similar things, so they won't be starting all over again.

New playmates
Get in touch with the school to arrange play dates with members of your child's class to help calm first day nerves.

GOOD PRACTICE

8 key principles

2
Explain why you are packing
If you start putting children's things into huge boxes, your child may think they are disappearing for good or getting thrown away. Explain that they are just being stored safely for the move and they will see them again soon.

3
Enlist your child's help
No matter your child's age, moving house feels like a decision made by adults. Help your child feel more in control by asking her to help with packing, for example, by putting her favourite things in a special box. Let her draw or write on the boxes to keep her busy and to show what's inside.

5
Pack up their old room last and unpack the new one first
Having a safe place with all their things at their new home will help your child feel more secure. Put your child's boxes into the moving van last so they are immediately to hand when you arrive.

7
Be upbeat
Even if your family's new changes are the result of a job loss or parental separation, be upbeat. Children pick up on and take in parents' feelings. If you feel ready to make the best of it, so will they.

8
Stick to a routine
Your child needs predictability to feel at home. Follow the usual bath and bedtime routine as soon as you're in your new place. This lets your child know that whatever else is changing, he can always rely on these things to happen.

"I love being with you."

No one is more important in your child's life than you, and she never feels more secure than when she has your undivided attention. These moments of quiet, undistracted togetherness can be some of the most treasured moments for both of you.

SCENARIO | **You and your child are walking along together, holding hands.**

SHE SAYS

"I love being with you."

Your child has a biological drive to be looked after. When this need is met, she forms a secure attachment. Until now, your child has shown that she feels safe with you by asking for hugs. Now she recognizes what love means from the many times she has heard you say it to her and she is old enough to express this feeling back to you.

SEE RELATED TOPICS

You're always too busy: pp.128–129
You promised: pp.168–169

YOU MIGHT THINK

"This is such special time together. This is what parenting is all about."

Being physically very close to you is a natural instinct for your child, before she goes on to learn how to be more independent. Sometimes it can feel like hard work to be the centre of your child's world, but it is a sign of secure attachment when she wants to be close to you like this.

WHAT SHE'S THINKING

"I feel safe and happy. I feel good when Mummy spends time just with me."

As much as your child is now doing many things to show her independence, she still needs to refuel through times with you and holding hands. Loving moments like these also release feel-good opioids in your child's brain, which will strengthen your bond.

HOW TO RESPOND

In the moment...

Respond in kind Reflect back the same loving words so she knows you appreciate her spontaneous surge of emotion. Don't respond with a joke or sarcasm as this may make her ashamed of expressing her honest feelings.

Give your full attention Be completely present and engaged when you are with your child and resist the temptation to use your phone around her. Otherwise she will think that other people are more important to you.

Comment on positive feelings Tell her when you notice she is happy so she learns that you don't only pay attention if she's upset. When you see her smiling and having fun tell her: "It's lovely that you're enjoying yourself."

In the long term...

Meet her eyes When your child asks for a cuddle or asks you to play with her, make eye contact to show her you are listening. She is saying "I love you" by sharing her emotions and games, so try to be attentive at these times.

Create opportunities Parents are busier than ever, so be mindful of the need for undistracted quiet times with your child. These can allow for intense emotional moments, which are when your child feels most connected to you.

"Why is the sky blue?"

As children learn more about the world, they try to make sense of what they discover. How you respond to their endless questions can help shape their wider understanding as well as help encourage their curiosity.

SCENARIO | **Your child is asking you a non-stop series of questions about the world while you're trying to get lunch ready.**

HE SAYS

"Why is the sky blue?"

At this age, children's brains are twice as active as an adult's and your child now has a vocabulary of more than 2,000 words at his disposal. This expands his ability to enquire and means he may ask you an average of 76 information-seeking questions per hour. He assumes you have the answer to everything.

YOU MIGHT THINK

"This is driving me mad. I don't know all the answers. Will there be any end to this?"

Dealing with a bombardment of unrelated questions can be exhausting. While parents want to deepen their child's curiosity, such questioning can be annoying. It's fine to say you don't know, and that you'd like to find out together.

WHEN CHILDREN ASK LOTS OF 'WHY' QUESTIONS, YOUR PATIENCE AND ENCOURAGEMENT CAN HELP THEM FOSTER A LIFE-LONG LOVE OF LEARNING.

WHAT HE'S THINKING

"I am learning so many new things. I just want to know even more."

Children are on a quest for information discovery – the world is an exciting place. Your child's brain is trying to join the dots between what he already knows. Such inquisition helps him to create neural pathways, so answers actively help to build connections in his brain. This age is also a time of learning the "to and fro" of conversation.

SEE RELATED TOPICS
That's so funny: pp.102–103
When I was little...: pp.114–115

HOW TO RESPOND

In the moment...

Stop momentarily and listen Often children will keep asking the same question if they don't get an answer that satisfies their curiosity. The answer doesn't have to be complicated. For instance, if your child asks: "Why are dogs furry?", you can answer "To keep them warm."

Welcome his queries When you give your child an answer, use an encouraging voice that shows you genuinely want to help him understand, not that you want him to be quiet. Praise him for wanting to learn.

Work out why he's asking Studies show that most of the time your child genuinely wants answers. But if you think he is asking questions to avoid doing something he doesn't want to do, such as tidying up, reply: "That's a good question. I can answer it while you collect your puzzle pieces".

In the long term...

Stretch his mind If your child asks about the colour of the sky, ask him why he thinks it's that colour. Even when he's only guessing, this gets his mind working in a more active way.

Explain there aren't always answers If your child asks about bigger questions, such as "What happens when we die?" or "Will we ever discover aliens?", tell him there are lots of different opinions, and sometimes there are no "right" answers.

"But I didn't hear you."

One of your biggest frustrations as a parent may be how many times you have to repeat yourself to get your child to do as you ask. Changing how you ask your child to do things can encourage her to cooperate without shouting or nagging.

SCENARIO | **Supper's ready, but despite shouting several times that it's time to come in from the garden, your child stays outside.**

SHE SAYS

"But I didn't hear you."

YOU MIGHT THINK

"I'm tired of nagging. She only seems to listen when she wants to."

At this age, children tend to concentrate on one activity at a time. When your child is absorbed, her brain may shut out anything that's not directly related to her activity. So even if she hears your shouts, she may not register their meaning.

You may feel your child is deliberately ignoring you and become angry because you think she is making your job as a parent harder. It may help you feel less frustrated if you understand that your child is likely to need help switching gears, or that you need to express yourself more clearly.

WHEN YOUR CHILD DOESN'T LISTEN, DON'T SHOUT LOUDER: SEEK HER COOPERATION.

SEE RELATED TOPICS
I'm just going to do it: pp.100–101
I don't want to tidy up: pp.148–149

WHAT SHE'S THINKING

"I'm having so much fun! I'm going to keep playing."

If she isn't entirely absorbed in her activity, your child may be choosing not to comply. She may also think she doesn't need to react if your request sounds like a question. Or, if you often repeat yourself, she may think she doesn't have to listen until you get angry.

HOW TO RESPOND

In the moment...

Be clear Instead of using questions such as "Can you please come inside now?", which may make your child think she has a choice, tell her simply what you'd like her to do. Say: "Dinner is ready now. It's time to come in."

Lower your tone Yelling can send your child's brain into fight-or-flight mode where she is less able to process what you are saying and act on it. Instead, use a firm, calm tone of voice.

Use eye contact If she keeps ignoring you, walk over to your child, get down on her level, and look her in the eye.

In the long term...

Seek cooperation Avoid criticizing your child for "never listening". Instead, appeal to her desire to cooperate. Acknowledge that she wants to keep playing, but talk about how she also wants dinner or she'll be hungry later.

Start a countdown If you feel your child is likely to resist, give her a countdown to let her know it will be time to finish soon. Advance warning will help her get used to the idea and make the transition easier.

"When I was little..."

While the memory centres in your child's brain are developing, he won't necessarily remember all the events he recalls now when he's older. But even though he may forget some things, such sharing of memories will boost his confidence and shape his view of the world.

SCENARIO | **Your child has surprised you by remembering an event during a holiday last summer, when he was 3.**

HE SAYS

"When I was little..."

YOU MIGHT THINK

"I thought he would have forgotten that by now."

Your child may remember that holiday today, but it is unlikely he will still recall it as he gets older. Researchers have found children need to know more language before they can permanently store recollections. At the moment, he will simply remember episodes without much context of where and when they happened or how he felt.

Adults forget most events from early life; this "infantile amnesia" is essential for brain development. Enjoy the fact that your child now recalls the lovely experiences you created; these are vital in making him feel secure and loved.

HELPING YOUR CHILD REMEMBER THE FUN TIMES, AS WELL AS THE CHALLENGES, WILL HELP HIM LEARN FROM THE PAST AND MAKE SENSE OF THE FUTURE.

WHAT HE'S THINKING

"I am a real person because I can remember."

In general, the older your child gets, the more he can remember. Although his current recollections may not be permanent, they will help form his sense of self and inform his role within the family. Even if an event happened last month, your child will say it took place "when he was little".

HOW TO RESPOND

In the moment...

Listen to the memories Pay attention and ask for more details. What was he thinking or feeling at the time? Such interaction helps him feel important and validates the way he experiences the world.

Fill in the gaps Children often need help retrieving memories at this age. Show him photos and retell the event as if it was a story that happened to him. This will also help him learn sequencing, a skill that helps with logical thinking and understanding cause and effect.

In the long term...

Make them interesting Children tend to remember the things they find most interesting. When you refer back to an event, choose questions that prompt memorable details, such as "Do you remember we went to the place where there were the pirate caves?" or "Whose ice cream was stolen by the seagull?".

Put memories in context The human brain tends to put more emphasis on negative memories. If your child tends to dwell more on these, for instance talking about falling off his bike on that holiday, acknowledge the memory. But also help him feel more positive with reminders of the fun times, too, so he builds a balanced picture of the world.

Show him how far he's come Talk about your child's memories so he takes pride in how far he's come in life. By pointing out that on holiday he was still learning to ride a bike but now rides it smoothly, you can remind him how he is capable of mastering new skills.

SEE RELATED TOPICS

Are you sad, Mummy?: pp.96–97
Why is the sky blue?: pp.110–111

"I give up."

Resilience is the ability to cope with challenges and bounce back from disappointment. To develop this skill, your child will need to find out what she is capable of through trial and error, and discover that persisting and learning from mistakes is the best way to improve.

SCENARIO | **Your child is trying to glue two boxes together to make a model. When it doesn't work, she storms off.**

SHE SAYS

"I give up."

YOU MIGHT THINK

"She needs to learn how to stick at things. But I hate seeing her so upset."

As a parent, it's natural to want to protect your child from difficulties and stress. But children need the time and space to find things challenging so they can practise their problem-solving and coping skills without you "fixing" their difficulties.

You may want to intervene as it feels uncomfortable to see your child distressed. You may also want to avoid her having a meltdown, which will be stressful for you. But by letting her finish this project on her own, you will be sending the message that you have faith she can do it without help.

SEE RELATED TOPICS
Was that good?: pp.164–165
I want it to be perfect: pp.172–173

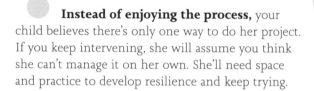

"If grown-ups have to help me it must mean I can't do it on my own."

Instead of enjoying the process, your child believes there's only one way to do her project. If you keep intervening, she will assume you think she can't manage it on her own. She'll need space and practice to develop resilience and keep trying.

HOW TO RESPOND

In the moment...

Reframe her thinking Ask your child to use her problem-solving skills to think of other ways to glue the boxes together. Or suggest she uses her creativity to think about how to turn it into a model that is different from the one she is trying to copy. Validate her efforts by saying: "I can see you're trying hard to do that".

Show her how far she's come Remind her of the things she wasn't able to do when she was little but can do now, for example, drawing pictures. Tell her that, with practice, she will get better at art projects too.

In the long term...

Don't "get in the way" Parents who hover over children and step in to fix their problems allow them to believe they can't do things on their own. Take a step back.

Give her lots of opportunities for free play Children learn to feel confident by feeling competent. At this age, this happens through giving children lots of real-world, hands-on play, which she chooses to do by herself. This will help her work out what she is capable of.

Encourage steps in the right direction Give your child targeted praise to show you are noticing the small progress she is making in learning new skills. Praise her flexibility and perseverance so she doesn't feel she has failed if she doesn't produce the "perfect" end result.

"I'm scared of the dark."

As your child's imagination takes flight and he becomes more aware of the wider world around him, your 4- and 5-year-old is starting to have fears that won't make much sense to you as an adult. One of the most common is fear of the dark.

SCENARIO | **Your child won't go to sleep because he's scared when his bedroom light is turned off.**

HE SAYS

"I'm scared of the dark."

YOU MIGHT THINK

"There's nothing to be afraid of. He's making excuses not to go to sleep now and vying for our attention."

Fear of the dark affects about half of children at this age. Although it's not helpful for modern parents, such fear once served a useful evolutionary role: at an age when children become more curious, and more physically able to explore the world, it stops them from wandering off at night and getting lost or, worse, eaten by a predator.

Usually such a fearful phase fades away within a few months. So, avoid dismissing your child's fears as a cry for attention. If his worries are dismissed or met with anger and frustration, he may become more scared.

CHILDREN CAN LEARN TO MANAGE THEIR FEARS OF THE UNKNOWN AND SOOTHE THEMSELVES WHEN GROWN-UPS SHOW THEM HOW.

WHAT HE'S THINKING

"If I want Mummy or Daddy, I won't be able to find them in the dark."

To your child, darkness feels like a big hole that could swallow him up. His fear is real because the darkness means he can't see familiar objects or environments that reassure him he is safe. What's more, his anxiety may make him alert to every creak in the house or noises from outside.

HOW TO RESPOND

In the moment...

Ask questions Find out exactly what your child is afraid of. Get him to talk about his feelings. Summarize and repeat back to him what he's saying, so he knows you have heard and understood. By helping to name his worries, he will feel more in charge.

Make his room a haven Your child's room needs to feel like a safe place, so never send him there as a punishment. A regular bedtime routine creates certainty of what comes next and when the room light goes off. Keep his door open so that there aren't any barriers between him and you, which will offer him extra comfort.

Adjust the lighting Buy your child a night-light, possibly in the form of a friendly animal, who will make him feel safe and will cast a warm glow within his room, so he can see his familiar things around him and feel reassured.

In the long term...

Check his viewing history Has your child seen older siblings or friends play older-age video games or has he seen scary films or heard ghost stories that are feeding his fears? Sometimes overhearing or catching a glimpse of TV news can also be enough to trigger worries in children this age.

Help him change the story At other times of the day, not before bedtime, read him a story in which he is the main character who overcomes a fear, such as a monster or the darkness. Find a story that can help him process fears during daylight hours.

SEE RELATED TOPICS

Sleep difficulties: pp.74–75
I've had a bad dream: pp.140–141

"I'm telling."

Parents want to encourage children to know the difference between right and wrong. However, some children can appoint themselves the enforcer of our rules, and not realize how unpopular tale-telling makes them with their peers.

SCENARIO | **Your child keeps coming to you to complain her playmate is not putting the lid back on the glue during a craft session.**

SHE SAYS

"I'm telling."

By this age, your child has learned about right and wrong from you and other grown-ups. She also craves your approval and thinks one of the best ways to get it is to prove to you that she knows all the rules, and will enforce them on your behalf.

" " YOU CAN HELP YOUR CHILD DEVELOP THE JUDGMENT TO KNOW WHEN TO ASK AN ADULT FOR HELP AND WHEN TO LET HER PEERS DECIDE.

YOU MIGHT THINK

"Why is she a tell-tale about such little things? She won't be very popular if she keeps doing this."

You may feel conflicted. On one hand you may be glad that your child is taking your rules on board; but, on the other, you may feel irritated that she is calling on you to intervene and arbitrate all the time. You may also be worried as you can see how annoying this will be to other children.

HOW TO RESPOND

In the moment...

Understand her motives Is she genuinely worried a rule has been broken or is she telling you to get attention and approval? If you suspect it's the latter, tell her: "I'm more interested in what you're up to."

Explain the difference between telling tales and telling Tell her that telling tales is when she wants to get another child into trouble. Telling is when she is letting you know another child is doing something that could hurt them or others.

Give her a bottom line Suggest she asks herself each time: "Is someone in danger? Is anyone crying?" If the answer is no, tell her she needs to let other children work out for themselves how to behave.

In the long term...

Don't reward the tale-teller If you reward your child by immediately rushing to discipline the other child, particularly in sibling disputes, your child will learn that telling tales gets results and she will do it more often.

Help her see how others see her Explain that other children won't want to play with her if they are always worried she's going to tell on them. Help her learn when is appropriate to get an adult involved by giving her a chance to practise her judgment about when to get grown-up help. For example, should she seek help when there's a row over who can be the unicorn in their game or when her friend has hurt her knee?

WHAT SHE'S THINKING

"I'm helping grown-ups if I tell them when others aren't doing what they've been told."

Your child may want your approval or your attention. She may also want to get back at her playmate for not playing by her rules, and thinks that getting a grown-up to intervene will give her the upper hand. Your child may be a stickler for rules, or she may not know what else to do when her play with another child is not going well.

SEE RELATED TOPICS

They say I'm a cry baby: pp.138–139
You can't come to my party: pp.152–153

Car journeys

Trips can be boring and difficult for children: it's a big ask to be physically restrained when you're full of energy. But by understanding where your child is developmentally, you can make travel more pleasant for the whole family.

Younger children do not yet understand the abstract concept of time – or how long an hour lasts – which can lead to repeated and exasperating "Are we there yet?" questions. They also do not yet understand time and distance, so they get frustrated when they don't know how long they will have to sit in a restricted seat for.

But, rather than viewing them as torments to be endured, long car journeys can offer great opportunities for parents and children to relax and have fun together.

That said, while they are still learning impulse control and patience, it's optimistic to expect every trip to be problem-free. Throw siblings into the mix and restlessness and rows can escalate in no time. So, being well prepared can help reduce the stress of travelling and make trips enjoyable.

1
Sort snacks and entertainment ahead
Before a big journey, ask your child what he would like to bring with him to help the time pass – his "bag of fun" – this could be an audio CD of a favourite books or songs, activity books, or cards.

4
Talk about seat belts
Some children hate being restrained by seat belts for long periods, but here compromise is not an option. Explain that wearing a seat belt keeps them safe in case of an accident. It may help to role-play car journeys in which children tell their toys why they must wear them.

6
Don't just rely on screens
If you believe screens will be helpful for a journey, it's still wise to set limits. Otherwise your child will expect to be entertained with gadgets at all times, even on short trips. Decide beforehand and tell him that you will let him watch a film or a TV episode at a certain point in the journey.

GOOD PRACTICE

8 key principles

2

Form a united front

Agree upfront how you and your partner want to handle common problems – sibling rows and requests for screens. Share any gripes beforehand, because seeing parental rows at such close range can be alarming for young children.

3

Interact with everyone

View journeys as a time to be together and chat, rather than ignore children until they get bored and start to protest. To make the journey go faster, play interactive games, such as I-spy or number plate spotting, or look out for landmarks, colours, and different-shaped clouds.

5

Deal with siblings separately

If sibling fighting gets serious, pull over and deal with it. Listen to each child's side and ask them how you can make the rest of the trip better. If you have adult help, take each child for a short walk to let off steam. Once they are back in the car, place a barrier between them to keep them out of touching distance.

7

Use simple markers of time

Depending on your child's age, his comprehension of time may be limited. So, use ways of relating the information about your journey in a way that your child can understand, such as "We'll be there after we've eaten lunch" or "…when the fields turn into a town".

8

Anticipate car sickness

Children may get car sick if they can't see out of the window or, if they are older, they are fixing their focus on a book or a gadget. Travel sickness arises when the inner ear senses motion, but the eyes and body don't, leading to feelings of nausea. Encourage your child to look out the window and distract them with talking games and stories.

TAILORED ADVICE

Age by age

2–3
YEAR-OLDS

PJs at the ready
If you've got a long car journey ahead, think about setting off in the evening or before dawn, so that your child sleeps for a lot of it.

Regular breaks
Look out for places to stop at parks, service stations, or playgrounds on the way.

4–5
YEAR-OLDS

Are we there yet? stickers
Make of game and see how many times he can resist the temptation of asking "Are we there yet?". Start with a page of stickers. Every time he asks, peel one off and put it on the dashboard where he can see it. At the end of the journey, he gets to keep all the stickers left.

Musical moments
Children this age love to show what they know. Play their favourite songs and then stop the music so that they can finish it off.

6–7
YEAR-OLDS

Map reading
Your child now has the spatial understanding to follow a map. To make the journey go more easily, give him a spare map and challenge him to follow the route with his finger. This will give him a sense of control over where he is going and allow him to work out how far you've come.

"You love her more."

Sibling rivalry is part of family life. It can never be avoided completely because children have a primitive need to secure their parents' care and protection. Understanding what children are really arguing over can help you respond better and reduce conflict.

SCENARIO | When your child doesn't get her own way about which film to watch, she says you love her sibling more.

Jealousy and rivalry continue throughout childhood, and children never completely outgrow it, so parents need to ensure they don't create more grounds for it. Sibling rivalry can show up in different ways:

● **Fighting for your attention** stems from the natural instinct not to lose out on food or protection. At the core of rivalry is the fact that brothers and sisters don't want any less of their parents' love.

● **Fighting over property** often occurs because younger children are behind older siblings in sharing skills. Children are also wired to seek out novelty, so a sibling's possessions may look more interesting. Older children may also be venting frustration, getting revenge for taking your attention, or asserting dominance.

See opposite for advice on spotting the warning signs, understanding the triggers, and how best to respond.

◄ SEE RELATED TOPICS ►
I hate her: pp.130–131
I never wanted a little brother: pp.134–135

" "

SIBLING RIVALRY OFFERS A SAFE TRAINING GROUND FOR LEARNING HOW TO DEAL WITH CONFLICT.

THE ROUTE TO FOLLOW

Assessing sibling rivalry

FIGHTING FOR YOUR ATTENTION

SIGNS

Jumping on you or timing disruptive behaviour for when you are with the other child.

Accusing you of favouritism and saying you love the other child more.

Asking who you love best.

TRIGGERS

Bedtimes when the older child is allowed to stay up later.

Rows over whether they can sit next to you at mealtimes.

Times when you are engaged with the other sibling.

Hearing praise of their sibling.

Feeling short-changed at bedtime.

RESPONSE

1. **Acknowledge her jealous feelings** and say you understand why she might have them, rather than gloss over jealousy or say there's no cause for it.

2. **Say you love your children for who they are:** tell her she is unique and you love her just as she is.

3. **Give time according to need** and explain why at certain times another child may need more time with you, for example, when they are ill.

4. **Set aside the same amount of special time** with Daddy and Mummy for each child every day.

5. **Don't compare:** even if you are praising their sibling in a positive way, it still sends the message that your children are in competition.

FIGHTING OVER PROPERTY

SIGNS

Tugs of war and grabbing their sibling's toys or possessions.

Physical fights and ruining games.

Using others' possessions without permission.

TRIGGERS

Boredom.

Desire to exercise power.

Jealousy of sibling and desire for revenge.

Wish to control how to play a game.

Frustration leading to destructive urges.

RESPONSE

1. **Don't try to identify the aggressor,** as one child will think they have lost and the other has won, triggering more hostility between them.

2. **Ask if they have any ideas** for how to resolve the conflict. If they think of some, give plenty of praise.

3. **Encourage games** which take teamwork, as children will bond more if they are striving for a common goal, for example, building a fort.

4. **Give them personal space,** such as a "sacred" shelf, where they can keep toys they don't want to share.

5. **Call regular family meetings.** To make sure every child feels heard, allow each to express their feelings about what's annoying them in a regular forum.

"I've lost teddy."

Your child now understands that he is a separate person from you, his parent. But he may still want the extra security of an object, such as a stuffed animal or a blanket, to comfort him when you're not with him.

SCENARIO | **You're trying to leave the house but your child refuses to come because he can't find his favourite soft toy.**

HE SAYS

"I've lost teddy."

YOU MIGHT THINK

"We need to go out now. Doesn't he need to grow out of having teddy?"

Between the age of 8 months and a year, your child began to understand that you couldn't always be with him. To bridge this gap, he adopted a favourite toy or object. This is special to your child because he can always have teddy with him.

However frustrating this situation is, teddy is an important part of his development and shows that he is working out ways to comfort himself. Addressing your child's need for teddy before he is ready may only make him want to hold onto it more.

CHILDREN HANG ON TO SPECIAL TOYS TO HELP THEM FEEL COMFORTED.

WHAT HE'S THINKING

"I've always had teddy. He makes me feel safe."

Your child's attachment to teddy is not a sign of insecurity or weakness. Instead, teddy is a companion who is helping your child make the transition from dependence to independence by helping him feel safe when he goes to bed or faces new situations.

HOW TO RESPOND

In the moment...

Tell him you understand When teddy goes missing, calmly tell him that you know teddy is important and he will have more time to look for him when he gets back. Reassure him teddy will stay safe in the meantime.

Set boundaries If you feel your child is using his cuddly toy as a reason to delay leaving the house, make it clear that you will still have to go out and he will have more time to find teddy when he gets back.

Divert him If your child is upset that he has to leave home without teddy, distract him with plenty of chat, songs, and games. Help your child use coping thoughts like "I'm strong enough" or "I can do this" to show him that he can still be strong without teddy.

In the long term...

Double up If your child takes teddy everywhere, there's always the risk that teddy will get lost. Buy an identical back-up in case teddy is mislaid, and then you also have a substitute when you have to wash the original. Swap them from time to time so both smell and feel the same.

Scale it down Most children will give up attachment objects by themselves by the age of about 6 as they start to see them as babyish. If you feel your child needs help to go it alone, suggest keeping teddy at home just for bedtimes. Or, if his security object is a blanket, see if he'll let you cut it into smaller squares to keep in his pocket.

SEE RELATED TOPICS
Can Mr Giraffe sit down, too?: pp.104–105
I'm scared of the dark: pp.118–119

"You're always too busy."

Children spell LOVE as T.I.M.E., so if your child feels you are too busy to give her your undivided attention, she can end up feeling rejected. Setting aside quality time together and giving her your undivided attention can make all the difference.

SCENARIO | **When your child asks you to come and play, you tell her you have to finish your online grocery shopping.**

SHE SAYS

"You're always too busy."

YOU MIGHT THINK

"I feel guilty that I can't play with her, but there's so much to do."

As soon as children enter our lives, they take up an extraordinary amount of time and effort, so it can be difficult to give them the time that you, and they, would like. But if you don't spend enough quality time together, your child may feel she isn't important to you.

In such moments, you're likely to feel both time pressure and emotional stress. You may also feel guilty, which can tip you into feeling overwhelmed. When you feel overloaded, you may lose empathy and become short-tempered with your child.

ASK FOR HELP FROM YOUR CO-PARENT AND FAMILY: IT TAKES A VILLAGE TO RAISE A CHILD, NOT ONE EXHAUSTED ADULT.

HOW TO RESPOND

In the moment...

(1)

Explain why Show your child what you are doing and explain why it's for the benefit of the whole family so she understands that there's a reason you aren't able to play with her right now.

(2)

Give her a time Set a specific time to play together after you've finished. In the meantime, ask her to plan an activity that you can both look forward to and honour your commitment.

In the long term...

Build in daily one-on-one time Even setting aside 15 minutes every day in which your child decides what you do together will send the message to your child that she is your priority. Make this special time regular, predictable, and phone-free so she is secure in the knowledge that you always have that time for her.

Don't let her think your phone or computer are more interesting Children may feel rejected if their parents are often glued to their devices. Try to use yours as little as possible when you are with your child.

Reduce your load Look for signs you are getting overloaded, such as feeling short-tempered or feeling resentment at how much you have to do. Take steps to refuel by setting aside time for yourself with a book, a bath, or seeing friends.

WHAT SHE'S THINKING

"Why does Mummy think other stuff is more important? I feel sad."

At this age, your child believes you decide how you spend your time. She doesn't yet fully understand you have jobs to do apart from being a parent, so may feel it's your choice not to play with her. Your emotions are also highly contagious, so she may "catch" your stress. This can show up as emotional outbursts, anger, or even withdrawal.

▶ SEE RELATED TOPICS ◀

Look what I've done!: pp.92–93
I love being with you: pp.108–109

"I hate her."

Siblings are wired to compete for your love and attention. Add to this their close proximity, and the fact they are still learning to control their emotions and impulses, and it's no surprise that, at times, your home can feel like a war zone.

SCENARIO | **Your younger child says he hates his 7-year-old sister after she banishes him from his room for being "annoying".**

HE SAYS
—
"I hate her."

While these extreme feelings are upsetting, it's normal for your child to feel a mix of conflicting emotions about his sibling. Sibling relationships are usually the most hostile because there is so much to fight over, including parents' love. These also tend to be children's most aggressive conflicts as siblings spend a lot of time together and aren't going anywhere, so are easy targets for their frustrations.

‟ ”

SIBLING RELATIONSHIPS TEACH CHILDREN LIFE-LONG SKILLS, SUCH AS SHARING.

◀ **SEE RELATED TOPICS** ▶
I'm going to explode: pp.98–99
She's so annoying: pp.146–147

YOU MIGHT THINK

"I hoped my children would grow up to be friends. How has it come to this?"

WHAT HE'S THINKING

"I feel hurt when she tells me to go away."

As rows usually start out of your view, it's hard to know whether one child is more to blame. You may also feel your older child should know better. But at 7, she doesn't understand that her brother's thought processes are still immature, so she gets cross when he can't play at her level.

Your younger child may feel anger, disappointment, and inferiority. His frustration has triggered his primal lower brain, so he can't be more specific about how he feels and sums it up as hatred. But this is fleeting: if his sister asked him to play now, he would accept.

HOW TO RESPOND

In the moment...

Acknowledge the full range of his feelings Show your child you have understood that he has a mix of emotions towards his sibling and these can change fast, for example, from anger when she won't play with him, to joy when they are playing well.

Encourage him to express what he means Help your child name the reasons for his anger so he can move beyond it. Tell him: "I hear that you're cross with your sister. I wonder if you're feeling sad that she told you she didn't want to play with you?"

Avoid labelling their relationship negatively Don't let your children hear you say they "don't get on" or they will define their relationship the same way.

In the long term...

Create chances for them to have fun together Get your children to collaborate on a project they can see to fruition, or try games where they team up against you. Having you as their common "enemy" brings them closer.

Teach your older child empathy Be understanding when your older child is upset so she learns to pass that kind behaviour along to her younger sibling.

"I feel sad."

Parents often imagine that children's lives are so carefree that they should be happy all the time, apart from the odd meltdown when they don't get their way. But your child will experience a range of emotions throughout her day.

SCENARIO | **As you walk home from school, you notice your child is quiet and seems downcast.**

SHE SAYS

"I feel sad."

YOU MIGHT THINK

"She's only little. What's she really got to be sad about?"

Children tend to experience feelings more intensely then adults, perhaps because they are more in touch with their primal brains. This means big and overwhelming feelings, such as sadness, may feel particularly intense. By talking openly, your child is showing her trust in you to listen.

You may feel worried to hear your child say she's feeling sad, because childhood is generally portrayed as a time without a care in the world. You may also feel you have somehow failed her because she's not having a 100 per cent happy childhood, which you feel is your responsibility.

HELP YOUR CHILD UNDERSTAND THAT EMOTIONS COME AND GO. THERE ARE WAYS TO MANAGE FEELINGS.

WHAT SHE'S THINKING

"Something made me feel bad today, and now my body feels heavy and I feel sad."

As your child gets older, she is able to identify and label her emotions. Now she is learning about cause and effect, she realizes that when something happens that she doesn't like it can affect how she feels. She has also worked out that sadness feels like a mix of being worried, feeling drained of energy, and more prone to tears.

HOW TO RESPOND

In the moment...

Be ready to listen Let your child express herself. If her sad feelings are not dealt with, they may surface in other ways – anger, tummy aches, or sleep problems. So, show her you're ready to listen. Squeeze her hand or offer her a cuddle straightaway; later, offer some special time.

Help her process the feelings Rather than ask lots of "why" questions, ask if she'd like to talk through the day and turn it into a story. If she does not want to dwell on painful moments, tell her she can skip over those. This retelling will help her piece her jumbled feelings together so she can make more sense of them.

Tell her feelings pass While your child may be sad now, it doesn't mean she'll feel sad all the time. Explain the difference between "I feel sad now" and "I am a sad person". Help her take the longer view, by asking her how she thinks she'll feel later, tomorrow, or next week.

In the long term...

Build awareness of feelings Train your child to pay attention to the feelings in her body when she experiences emotions. Show her how doing something physical – playing a game outside or running – can help shift her emotional state to a new one.

Explore your own feelings Children can be emotional barometers for a family. Are there any particular worries that may be impacting on your child's happiness? If you find yourself becoming annoyed with her for expressing this sadness, it may help to talk to friends and family to help you figure out your feelings.

SEE RELATED TOPICS

I'm going to explode: pp.98–99
I want it to be perfect: pp.172–173

"I never wanted a little brother."

First-born children are the only children in a family who start life enjoying the exclusive attention of their parents. It can turn your elder child's life upside down when you bring home a sibling who he will view mainly as a rival for your love.

SCENARIO | **You are delighted to have just welcomed your second child to the family.**

HE SAYS

"I never wanted a little brother."

While you may have had your second baby partly to give your child the gift of a companion, at first he is unlikely to see it this way. First-borns are used to believing the world revolves around them so can find it particularly hard to adjust to sharing you.

SEE RELATED TOPICS

I love being with you: pp.108–109
You love her more: pp.124–125

YOU MIGHT THINK

"This isn't the happy family I'd planned."

WHAT HE'S THINKING

"I don't want to share Mummy and Daddy with anyone."

Now your child realizes that the new baby is a permanent arrangement, you may be shocked and disappointed when he tells you he wants to send the baby back. You may also feel guilty that you're no longer able to spend as much time with your elder child as before.

Your child is likely to be angry with you for bringing a rival home. The only upside he has been told about – that he'll get a playmate – will be shaken by the fact that, at first, all the baby does is eat, sleep, and take your attention away from him.

HOW TO RESPOND

In the moment...

Don't tell him how he's supposed to feel Let your child talk about his feelings and worries so you can address them directly. Show you have understood and that it's safe to express himself by saying: "I know life has changed a lot and you'd like it to go back to how it was."

Give him other ways to express his emotions Let your child express his feelings through drawings if he can't find the words, or with his toys, even if this means he uses force to relieve his frustration.

In the long term...

Make special time Do all you can to stay engaged with your elder child. For example, carry your newborn in a sling so you have your hands free to play with him.

Ask for help Ease this difficult period by discussing with your partner and family members how they can help your older child feel special – and arrange one-on-one times just for them.

Don't make it all about the baby Avoid using the baby as a reason why you can't spend time with your child, or making him feel that his main role is to help. Praise his achievements and tell him the baby is fascinated by him, for example: "Look how the baby is watching you play."

Dealing with a poorly child

Children get lots of minor illnesses in their early years as they build up their immunity. Whatever the ailment, help your child build physical and psychological resilience by caring for them with sympathy and practicality.

When your child falls sick, it's natural for worry and protectiveness to kick in. It can often be hard to assess how sick your child is when she says: "I don't feel well" or 'My tummy hurts" because she doesn't yet have all the words to describe how she feels.

Because parents want to be as kind as possible, they may also wonder about whether the usual routines and expectations of behaviour should still apply during short periods of illness.

If you're in any doubt about how ill your child is, seek professional advice.

> **HELP YOUR CHILD STAY CALM ABOUT AN ILLNESS BY BEING CALM AND REASSURING YOURSELF.**

1
Model a positive attitude to health
Children take cues from the way you handle illness. When you're ill, model resilience and care for yourself.

4
Use brave talk
Tell your child that while her body is working hard at getting better, she can help by being a brave patient and following your advice.

7
Stick to boundaries
As far as possible, keep family rules in place – for instance, no hitting siblings and a limit on screen-time. If rules do slip, return to your usual expectations step-by-step.

9
Remember siblings
If a child is ill for a while, make sure any other siblings are not feeling left out. Arrange special times to focus on them.

↓
GOOD PRACTICE
10 key principles

2
Talk about getting better
Discuss with your child about how strong her body is and how good it is at healing itself. If you need to talk to others about her illness, do so out of her earshot.

3
Check guidelines
Not every illness means keeping your child off school. Ask yourself: "Is my child too ill to join in activities?" "Does she have something contagious?" "Would I take a day off if I had it?" If the answer is yes to any of these, keep her home.

5
Stay neutral
Listen when your child says she has an ache or pain. But try not to get overanxious or emotional when she complains as this may reinforce inappropriate attention seeking.

6
Give lots of cuddles
When your child is sick, he may regress to more infantile behaviour and want to be more attached to you. Respond accordingly.

8
Work out priorities
If you work, you are entitled to ask for emergency discretionary leave, either unpaid or as a day's holiday to care for a sick child.

10
Share the load
Even when both partners work, the job of caring for a sick child still tends to fall on mothers, with 72 per cent of women saying they are the most likely to take time off work to look after ill offspring. When illness strikes, talk about splitting nursing duties. Can you and your partner divide the day so that one goes in late and the other comes home early? Is it easier for one of you to make up the lost time by working over a weekend?

TAILORED ADVICE
Age by age

2–3
YEAR-OLDS

Body language
Young children may express emotional difficulties via their bodies. Watch out for patterns in headaches or tummyaches.

Out of bed
Young children can run fevers and simultaneously want to run around. If you can't keep them in bed, don't worry.

4–5
YEAR-OLDS

Easy does it
After an illness, some children may feel nervous about returning to school. Reassure them that it will feel the same as before.

Root cause
Studies have found that at this age children have limited understanding of the causes of illness. Make it clear that being ill is not your child's fault.

6–7
YEAR-OLDS

Doctors and nurses
Research found that when 6-year-olds are ill they can believe medical treatment is a kind of punishment unless someone explains how it helps them get better.

It's catching
By 7, children become aware that some illness can be "caught" from other people. Let them know what kind of illness they have.

"They say I'm a cry baby"

Children start to cry less at about the age of 2 when they can start to use words to express how they feel and learn to regulate their emotions better. However, some children are temperamentally more sensitive and more prone to tears.

SCENARIO | **Your child tells you his classmates don't want to play with him because they say he's a cry baby.**

HE SAYS

"They say I'm a cry baby."

YOU MIGHT THINK

"Why can't he toughen up?"

Your child may not yet realize that while crying gets sympathy from adults, his peers find it annoying. When he bursts into tears, it interrupts the flow of their game and adults tend to intervene. Then, his peers get angry with him for "spoiling" the fun.

Due to the long-held images of what it means to be a "man", if you have a son you may unconsciously want him to cry less and be tougher. Even if these are not your beliefs, you may still worry that's what others expect. So, you may want your child to mask his feelings so his classmates don't call him "a wimp" or "a cry baby".

DON'T SEE IT AS YOUR ROLE TO MAKE YOUR CHILD DEVELOP A THICK SKIN BUT TO HELP HIM LEARN TO MANAGE HOW HE RESPONDS.

WHAT HE'S THINKING

"When I get upset, my tears come out. I can't help it."

Your child may simply find it harder to control his feelings than other children do. Research has found that 15–20 per cent of children come into the world with a more sensitive temperament. They often start by being more easily startled as babies and may grow into children who are more easily distressed.

HOW TO RESPOND

In the moment...

Help him manage the tears Show your child how breathing slowly can calm him down. Help him practise – breathing in through his nose and out through his mouth. Such breathing slows the release of adrenaline and will help him stay calmer and more logical.

Be gender neutral Don't tell him not to cry because he's a "big boy". Boys need to be able to express their feelings, just as much as girls.

Help him keep perspective While encouraging him to talk about how he feels, train him to keep minor upsets in perspective. Explain that everyone has conflicts with friends – it's part of the ups and downs of relationships.

Don't deny his emotions Male role models can also show it's OK for boys to cry, but talk about how it can be more comforting and stress-relieving to shed tears among close family and friends than among children who may not understand.

In the long term...

Teach him other coping strategies Show him how to anticipate situations that might make him cry, such as losing a game, not being allowed to join in, or being teased. Suggest he distracts from his strong feelings by thinking of a fun memory, counting to ten, or imagining being surrounded by a magical and protective force.

SEE RELATED TOPICS
I'm scared of the dark: pp.118–119
I'm telling: pp.120–121

"I've had a bad dream."

Although parents wish their children sweet dreams, most children will have the occasional nightmare. At the age of 4 and 5, about three-quarters of children have frightening dreams from time to time, with some having as many as one or two a week.

SCENARIO | **Your child has woken up in the night distressed, saying she was lost and being chased by a monster.**

SHE SAYS

"I've had a bad dream."

Children experience more rapid eye movement (REM) sleep – a type of deep sleep in which dreaming occurs – than adults. Dreams are a sign of increasing sophistication in the brain, building up a bigger memory bank, and processing more fears as she learns more about the world.

YOU MIGHT THINK

"Why is she being woken by these bad dreams? Is something bothering her?"

Seeing your child distressed is upsetting, heightened by the fact you're startled awake in the middle of the night. Bad dreams can result from watching something scary, from a troublesome worry, and are more common at times of upheaval – such as starting a new school or family discord.

SEE RELATED TOPICS
I'm scared of the dark: pp.118–119
I wet the bed: pp.158–159

" "

TELL YOUR CHILD IT'S POSSIBLE TO CHANGE THE STORY OF A BAD DREAM – AND GIVE IT A HAPPY ENDING.

WHAT SHE'S THINKING

"Did the things in my dream really happen?"

Since your child's still developing the ability to tell the difference between real and imaginary, nightmares feel as if they really happened. She doesn't know that such bad dreams are created in her own imagination as her brain tries to process what's gone on in her day.

HOW TO RESPOND

In the moment...

Stay calm and reassure Children can find it hard to calm down after a bad dream. Cuddle her and in a soothing way say: "How scary that must have felt. It's all over now. It wasn't real." Keep interaction brief, though, so she quickly falls back to sleep.

Encourage her to stay where she is Rather than let her come into bed with you, try to calm your child so she goes back to sleep in her own room and learns to soothe herself in her own surroundings.

In the long term...

Talk about her feelings in the light of day If she talks more about her emotions when she is with you, it may allow her to process her experiences during the daylight hours when it feels less disturbing, and a reason may emerge. She may like to draw about it, too.

Help her get enough sleep A consistent bedtime routine, a cuddle, and a favourite book before bed will help your child feel more secure and relaxed for a good night's sleep.

Check what she's watching Your child's nightmares may stem from seeing films, video games, or news items that are too old for her. Be careful to screen out any images she is not ready for.

"I didn't do it."

From time to time, nearly all children will tell untruths, omit details, or exaggerate. By understanding the reasons behind lying and responding in the most appropriate way, parents can prevent this necessary developmental phase from turning into a habit.

SCENARIO | You see your child push his friend over, but your child denies it.

Honesty is valued highly by adults. But although you may think of lying as always being bad, it helps to see it as a landmark in your child's thinking skills. In order to tell the difference between what is true and false, your child has to develop "theory of mind", or the ability to put himself in other people's shoes.

There are two main types of lie:

● **Anti-social lies** are told by children to get themselves out of trouble after they have done something wrong, to escape being punished for breaking rules, or to cast the blame on others.

● **Pro-social lies** are untruths told by omitting information, and not giving the whole truth, rather than telling a deliberate fib. They are also told to spare the feelings of others.

It helps to understand the difference because each needs a different response. See opposite for how they compare.

> IF YOU CATCH YOUR CHILD LYING, EMPHASIZE THAT THERE ARE BETTER WAYS TO SOLVE THE PROBLEM.

SEE RELATED TOPICS
But I didn't hear you: pp.112–113
She's so annoying: pp.146–147

THE ROUTE TO FOLLOW

Assessing a lie

ANTI-SOCIAL LIES

SIGNS

His story doesn't add up or make sense,
and is not consistent.

He uses more words than needed to try to convince you.

The physical and mental stress of making up a lie
may make his voice higher pitched.

TRIGGERS

A fear of getting in trouble.

Breaking a rule.

Wanting to get someone else in trouble.

Trying to avoid blame for something he has
done wrong.

RESPONSE

1. **Understand** the development behind it. Children up to 3 or 4 may not understand the difference between fantasy and reality, or may be indulging in wishful thinking.

2. **Point out** that when he tells the truth, you have a better chance of helping him to resolve an issue.

3. **Make it clear** that you will approve more if he is honest and that it's the best way to make amends.

4. **Make telling the truth** one of your family values, and explain how lying can stop others believing him even when he is telling the truth.

5. **Don't discipline too harshly** If children have done something they know they shouldn't, they're more likely to lie if they are terrified of the consequences.

PRO-SOCIAL LIES

SIGNS

Other parents asking you about things
your child has bragged about.

He gives short or incomplete answers to questions.

He gives contradictory answers according to the
question because he is trying to keep you happy.

TRIGGERS

Wanting to avoid the inconvenience of adults'
rules, for example, lying about completing
homework to go out to play.

Wanting to impress peer and parents.

Trying to save another's feelings; such "white lies"
can be the sign of a socially aware child.

RESPONSE

1. **Explain the consequences.** If your child has said he's getting a puppy but isn't, say you know he'd like one, but others won't believe him if he keeps lying.

2. **Role model honesty,** as if your child hears you tell a "white lie" he'll learn it's socially acceptable to do so.

3. **Help build your child's self-worth.** Some children may tell lies or exaggerate facts about themselves if they don't feel quite good enough about themselves.

4. **Check your expectations** are not too high. If your child seems to have deliberately hidden a test mark from you say: "It seems important for you to get good marks. Do you worry about disappointing us?"

5. **Say you trust them.** Children are more likely to be honest if they have a good reputation to live up to.

"I had an accident."

Even if your child is mainly dry in the day, there may be times when she still wets her knickers. Daytime wetting affects about 1 in 7 children aged 4 but reduces to 1 in 75 over the age of 5. It may happen only in the day or along with bedwetting.

SCENARIO | **Your child keeps wetting her knickers during the day.**

SHE SAYS

"I had an accident."

Children need to urinate between four and seven times a day. If your child has been dry before, there could be a physical reason for her accidents, such as a urinary tract infection, which means she is weeing in smaller but more frequent amounts.

SEE RELATED TOPICS
I didn't do it: pp.142–143
I wet the bed: pp.158–159

MOST CHILDREN WILL HAVE ACCIDENTS. BE SUPPORTIVE SO ANY EMBARRASSMENT DOESN'T UNDERMINE THEIR CONFIDENCE.

YOU MIGHT THINK

"I thought she would have grown out of this by now. Other kids will make fun of her."

WHAT SHE'S THINKING

"There's so much to do, I just forget to go to the loo."

You may be annoyed that she did not take herself to the loo in good time. And may also wonder if you should put her in pull-ups or nappies. But, if you make her feel more babyish or ashamed, it's likely to worsen the problem.

Children can have fears about going to the loo: some think they are smelly or worry about getting locked in, while others are self-conscious around others. But maybe she is so busy that she is just leaving it too late.

HOW TO RESPOND

In the moment...

Find out what's wrong Try to get to the bottom of why her knickers got wet again today. Perhaps role-play her day to find out why she's not getting to the toilet in time. If something's causing her to feel stressed, it'll be harder for her to manage her bodily functions as well.

Don't say wet Use the term "not dry" rather than "wetting yourself", which may trigger feelings of shame.

In the long term...

Reward dry days Set up a star chart with small rewards for getting to the toilet in time and for having dry knickers at the end of the day.

Help her slow down Get her to take her time when she wees. This will help the tap-like muscle – the sphincter – at the base of the bladder open fully to empty completely.

Get your child to drink more Rather than getting your child to drink less, encourage her to drink six to eight glasses of water-based drinks throughout the day, so her bladder fills properly and sends stronger signals that it needs to be emptied.

"She's so annoying."

At this age, your child has moved on from parallel play – playing side by side – to interacting more directly with his playmates. While he is still learning the rules, be prepared for him to have conflict with his peers more frequently.

SCENARIO | **While playing in a sandpit, your child pushes his friend in a row over how they should play.**

HE SAYS

"She's so annoying."

YOU MIGHT THINK

"This is embarrassing! I don't want him to be branded a troublemaker."

Parents want their children to play nicely. But while they are learning to express what they want verbally, most children this age will sometimes use some kind of force to get what they want. Studies show that boys and girls can use a range of physical strategies to establish dominance and make the game go their way.

You may feel embarrassed if there are other adults present. While you may feel you should intervene, he will learn best if he handles this himself. Tiffs are usually quickly forgotten if both want to continue their game.

CHILDREN ARE THE BEST AT TEACHING EACH OTHER HOW TO GET ALONG. WITH LOTS OF PLAYTIME, THEY MOSTLY LEARN TO WORK IT OUT.

WHAT HE'S THINKING

"I don't know what else to do when my friend says she won't play my way."

Your child is still working out the to-and-fro of social interaction and the rules of sharing, taking turns, and compromise. He is only just starting to understand that others have feelings and that if he won't share, or wants to be in charge all the time, his friend won't want to play any more.

HOW TO RESPOND

In the moment...

Stand back and observe You will find that, if they were having fun, children are often motivated to come up with a solution for themselves. Even if they don't, praise them for listening to each other and taking steps in the right direction.

Don't play referee If your child asks you to arbitrate, accept that you won't get to the bottom of what happened. Instead suggest both children explain in their own words why they are unhappy so they both feel heard.

Remind your child of other people's feelings Rather than tell your child off for not playing well, help him appreciate his friend's perspective. For example, tell him: "I don't think she liked it when you took the spade from her."

In the long term...

Make an assessment Conflict is a normal part of learning social interaction at this age, but if your child seems to have more trouble restraining his impulse to get his own way, he may need more help regulating his emotions or understanding the right way to react in social situations.

Take it outside When children have a friend over to play, they have more fun and squabble less if most of their play is outdoors. That's because there is less to argue over and they bond more when they discover and explore new things together.

▸ SEE RELATED TOPICS ◂

I'm telling: pp.120–121
You can't come to my party: pp.152–153

"I don't want to tidy up."

Play is key to your child's emotional and intellectual development. The downside of play at this age is the trail of puzzle pieces, Lego bricks, play figures, and crayons that are left behind. Your child may need help to learn how to help clear up.

SCENARIO | **The living room floor is littered with toys but your child does nothing when you ask her to help put them away.**

SHE SAYS

"I don't want to tidy up."

When your child is absorbed in playing, it makes sense for her to have all her playthings spread out but still within easy reach. Then, she can stretch her imagination and create new games by using them together – making a house out of bricks for her play figures and animals, for instance.

YOU MIGHT THINK

"She constantly creates chaos for me to clean up. It's exhausting. Doesn't she care about all of her things?"

While you may prefer more order and less chaos at home, your child doesn't, like you, see the "mess" as annoying. Most adults like to have "homes" for things to be put away. Your child will need to learn this over time.

SEE RELATED TOPICS
Look what I've done!: pp.92–93
I don't want to: pp.156–157

HOW TO RESPOND

In the moment...

Join in Tidying up all her toys alone will feel overwhelming to your child at this age. So, make it clear it's a job that you are doing together.

Give guidance Instead of saying "tidy up", be specific about how you want her to help: "Please put all the dinosaurs into their box" or ask her to pick up her blue crayons, while you pick up the red ones.

Make tidying up part of the fun Invent a special tidying up song or choose an up-tempo playlist as an energetic backing track. Or set the kitchen timer to challenge her to race to see who can put the most Lego back in their box and be Tidying Up Champion today.

In the long term...

Show the benefits Children at this age are caught between following their own wants and wanting to help adults. Help your child see that by clearing up, she will have space to run around, will be keeping her toys safe, and will know where to find them tomorrow.

Make it regular Schedule clean-up time at the same time every day – perhaps the interval just before dinner – to get kids into the habit.

WHAT SHE'S THINKING

"I don't want my toys to disappear. And there are so many on the floor, I don't know where to start."

Your child may feel she is being asked to break up the world she has just created. Being told to put away all these toys is hard for her. She needs plenty of prompts about tidy-up time approaching to transition from one activity to the next.

A FAMILY HOME IS NOT A SHOW HOUSE. IF YOUR CHILD IS HELPING TO MAKE IT LESS MESSY, YOU'RE ON THE RIGHT PATH.

"You have to."

All parents want their children to have a good group of friends, so it can be worrying to hear your child drive other children away by using domineering behaviour. He may need your help to consider others' feelings.

SCENARIO | **On a play date, you overhear your child telling his friend he must play the game by his rules.**

HE SAYS
—
"You have to."

Children already feel told what to do a lot by grown-ups. So when a playmate tries to take charge, they find it irritating and so stop wanting to play with him. Research has found that being able to play collaboratively and let others take turns are key skills for making and keeping friends.

SEE RELATED TOPICS
I'm telling: pp.120–121
She's so annoying: pp.146–147

YOU MIGHT THINK

"I want him to stand up for himself, but if he keeps being bossy, he won't have any friends."

WHAT HE'S THINKING

"Why won't he do it my way?"

You may worry that your child is missing the social skills to be able to play well. While some parents might see such dominance as a sign of future confidence, there is a difference between leadership (making others want to follow) and bossiness (telling others what to do).

Your child may still be learning that others have different views and how to recognize signs of annoyance. He is also now working out where he fits into the social hierarchy, so he may be testing how much other children will do what he tells them.

HOW TO RESPOND

In the moment...

Be sure about intervening This dialogue may just be part of the push and pull of a game, so don't jump in unless he is telling the other child what to do all the time or the other child is getting frustrated or upset.

Have a quiet word If his behaviour is in danger of ruining the play date, take your child to one side and point out how the other child might be feeling. Suggest he asks what his playmate thinks so he considers other people's points of view.

In the long term...

Give him practice Good games all need a certain level of give and take. Role-play scenarios with toys and ask him to imagine what different characters are feeling.

Help him to spot clues Tell your child to listen out for himself saying words like: "You have to" or "You shouldn't". Come up with a secret signal – such as a throat-clearing "ahem" – if you spot him slipping into this again so he starts to become aware.

Model gentle behaviour If it's not a case of your child being inflexible or failing to understand the give and take of play, could he be copying behaviour of adults or is he being bossed around by older siblings?

"You can't come to my party."

Your child is now starting to make firmer friendships and form social groups, but she will also be starting to have conflicts. Birthday parties can be opportunities for her to wield social power, to include or exclude others.

SCENARIO | **You overhear your child telling a classmate that she's not invited to her birthday party.**

SHE SAYS

"You can't come to my party."

YOU MIGHT THINK

"Why is she being so mean? I don't want her to be seen as a bully."

Children's friendships move fast; classmates fall in and out of favour depending on whether they had a good game that day. Your child may feel her party makes her more socially powerful – and she's using it to get others to play games by her rules.

Children are still learning empathy. Unless you point it out, she won't realize that her words can be just as painful as hitting. You may feel shocked that she is flexing her social muscles, but one mean remark does not mean it's bullying.

MODEL KINDNESS TO OTHERS. EXPLAIN HOW CRUEL WORDS CAN HURT AS MUCH AS HITTING.

WHAT SHE'S THINKING

"It's my party and I am in charge. I decide who should be there."

Your child is still working out her place in the classroom social pecking order. She knows other children want to go to parties and that, as the birthday girl, she has some say about who is on the guest list. Unless she learns she is being unkind, she will use this fact to increase her social power.

HOW TO RESPOND

In the moment...

Ask her reasons Out of the hearing of other children, understand why your child has chosen not to invite this classmate. Listen to her and find out if there are more long-term friendship difficulties that need dealing with.

Point out the hurt Ask your child to imagine what it would feel like if someone told her in front of others that she wasn't invited to a party. Would she feel sad? Hurt? You need to help her understand that her actions and words in this instance are unkind.

In the long term...

Keep perspective If you build the party up for weeks, your child may develop an exaggerated sense of its importance. Children this age can find it hard to regulate their excitement and may not be able to resist using the guest list to get others to do as she wants.

Finalize the guest list as late as possible Children's friendships change as they grow and develop. The child who was a constant playmate two months ago may not still be playing with them in the weeks before the party.

Don't give your approval Some parents may think this kind of social confidence is a sign that their child is popular. But if you don't tell her why it's wrong to treat others like this, she may think it's acceptable to keep excluding others.

▶ SEE RELATED TOPICS ▶
I didn't do it: pp.142–143
She's so annoying: pp.146–147

Birthday parties

What used to be simple affairs, built around musical bumps, cutting the birthday cake, and jelly and ice cream have become more elaborate and expensive events. In the last 20 years, spending on parties has rocketed.

Your child's birthday is a significant date in your calendar – and the reason for a party to celebrate. As the date approaches it's helpful to talk to your child about the true meaning of birthdays.

Because of the simple way young children see cause and effect, research has found that before the age of 6, almost half of young children believe it's having a party on the birthday itself that makes them a year older. They don't understand that their birthday marks the passing of a whole year. So, explain it's not the party that makes them a new age; they get older because of the days that have past and what they have learned.

Mark the occasion by looking together over your child's drawings and family photos from the last year to show him how far he's come in the past 12 months.

In terms of length of parties, aim for 1–2 hours depending on your child's age.

1
Have a pre-party chat
From the age of 4 or so, children may want a party based around a favourite TV show, book, or film. Don't plump for a theme too far in advance, though, as their interests.

4
Pick your time
Choose the window when your child is at his most alert and even-tempered; it's best to work around nap times for younger children.

7
Do it your child's way
Birthday parties are designed to make the birthday girl or birthday boy feel special. The best way to do that is to organize a party that's just for your child. It's his wishes and his interests that you want to plan around, not those of others.

> ## YOUNG CHILDREN WILL ENJOY A PARTY MUCH MORE IF IT'S PITCHED AT JUST THE RIGHT DEVELOPMENTAL LEVEL FOR THEM.

GOOD PRACTICE

10 *key principles*

2
Consider the guest list
To decide how many guests would make the party fun and enjoyable for your child, follow the "age plus one" rule. Though once children start school, that may have to bend somewhat.

3
Ask older children to be sensitive
If your child does not want to invite everyone in his class, ask him to be sensitive by not talking about his party in front of those who are not invited.

5
Prepare for meltdowns
Kids tend to have fewer conflicts with peers when they play outside. Invite friends (plus families) to a picnic in a park. Too many children inside can be overwhelming for young children.

6
Ask parents to help
Children aren't always ready to separate from their parents during social events. On the invite, ask parents to stay so that everyone knows what to expect.

8
Leave present opening for afterwards
Until the age of 3 some children may not understand that they have to leave the gifts they've brought with them and can't take them home. Collect up presents on arrival so that they don't distract from the fun.

9
Help them be a good host
Just before the party, talk to your child about being kind and welcoming to every guest, and not just paying attention to their closest friends.

10
Stay grounded
If you recall your own childhood parties, you may remember the best moments were about the fun you had with your friends, not the venue or how much money the party cost.

Age by age

2–3
YEAR-OLDS

Stagger gifts
Give your child a few presents to open after the event but hold back others to give throughout the year.

Keep it simple
A theme is easiest for 2-year-olds – water, sand, or plasticine – to meet their need for parallel play. But by 3, children are ready for circle activity games.

4–5
YEAR-OLDS

School class dilemmas
Either ask a small group which is less than half the class, or the whole class. And have plenty of group games prepared.

Go ballistic!
Kids this age love balloons because they float and move slowly, allowing them to manipulate them better.

6–7
YEAR-OLDS

VIPs only
As peer groups become more important, your child will want more say in the theme and who's on the guest list.

Choosing favourites
Children now prefer parties based around skills they are particularly good at and can show off to their friends – popular choices are football, swimming, dancing, or art.

"I don't want to!"

Your child is likely to be developing control of her body faster than she is learning the vocabulary to express her feelings, so she may lash out if she is angry or frustrated. As upsetting as this behaviour might be, keep your own emotions under control.

SCENARIO | Your child kicks out at you when you tell her it's time to stop watching TV and come upstairs for a bath.

SHE SAYS

"I don't want to!"

Kicking, hitting, and biting are a normal part of your child's development. Your child wants to try being independent by asserting her will, but when she doesn't get her way, the emotional part of her brain kicks in. As she gets physically stronger, she also experiments with using force.

YOU MIGHT THINK

"I'm shocked. How could she hurt me like this?"

In such a high-stress situation, your own fight-or-flight instinct is likely to be triggered. You may also be so taken aback that you want to shock her into compliance by hitting back. Though it feels like your child is being deliberately aggressive, she is trying to tell you something.

STAYING CALM BUT RESPONDING FIRMLY WHEN YOUR CHILD LASHES OUT WILL HELP TRAIN HER TO REGULATE HER EMOTIONS.

WHAT SHE'S THINKING

"I love Mummy. Now she is sad because I have kicked her."

Your child is learning that her actions have effects, kicking is wrong, and you have feelings too. So when she calms down and the logical part of her brain regains control, she feels remorseful. She may be shocked that you are upset because at this age children believe their parents are invulnerable.

SEE RELATED TOPICS
It's not fair!: pp.180–181
But I'm not tired: pp.216–217

HOW TO RESPOND

In the moment...

Don't meet hitting with more hits Talk slowly and gently, telling her to take big, slow breaths and calm down to help her regain control of her feelings. Rather than saying "No", which will enrage her more, try to respond without anger. Suggest an alternative such as "Let's see what Daddy is doing" to put her brain into another gear.

Talk it through When your child has calmed down and is able to use her rational brain again, tell her you understand she was frustrated with you, but kicking is always the wrong way to show her anger. Repeat the ground rule: "In our family, we do not kick".

Regain your bond as soon as possible When she is calm, have a cuddle but explain how her behaviour made you feel so she learns that other people having feelings. Explain that it's OK to be angry, but not to hurt others.

In the long term...

Tell her to use words When she is feeling calm, help her point out or draw where she feels anger in her body. Help her learn words to express this so that she can let you know when she starts to feel like lashing out. She may want help describing it, such as a pan boiling over or a volcano erupting.

Get a routine Children are more likely to react physically when they are tired or hungry, have too much sugar, or are overstimulated with too much screen-time or excitement. Set up a predictable schedule for sleeping, playing, and mealtimes so she knows what to expect and is less likely to kick up a fuss.

"I wet the bed."

Staying dry through the night is the last stage of toilet training. It takes many types of development to come together for this to happen, so children reach this point at different ages. Four out of ten 4-year-olds and a quarter of 5-year-olds wet the bed.

SCENARIO | **Your child has wet the bed for the third time this week.**

HE SAYS

"I wet the bed."

There are many reasons your child may be wetting the bed. His nervous system may not yet be wired well enough for his bladder to send a wake-up call to his brain or he may have a smaller bladder. If you or your partner wet the bed in childhood, he has a 25 per cent higher risk of doing the same.

TRUST THAT YOUR CHILD WILL GET THERE. KEEP HIS SELF-CONFIDENCE INTACT WHILE HE LEARNS TO BE DRY AT NIGHT.

YOU MIGHT THINK

"It's exhausting to change the bed in the middle of the night. When is he going to grow out of this?"

Despite your frustrations, try to be understanding. Knowing that most kids grow out of wetting the bed is little comfort when nights are broken and there's extra washing, but bedwetting is out of your child's control so be supportive.

SEE RELATED TOPICS
I've had a bad dream: pp.140–141
I've had an accident: pp.144–145

"I feel ashamed. I don't want anyone else to know."

Bedwetting can dent your child's self-worth – he may feel it's babyish and feel ashamed of the upset it causes – so he'll need plenty of comfort, one-on-one time, and reassurance that he will grow out of it. Anxiety can also trigger bedwetting.

HOW TO RESPOND

In the moment...

Stay upbeat Praise your child for his dry nights. Be matter of fact about his wet ones. All you need to say is: "Let's get you up and change these sheets."

Give him a positive mind-set While sorting his bed, talk to him about being "dry" and "not dry" rather than being "wet", which may trigger feelings of shame. If you or your partner wet the bed as children, let him know because he will see that you've grown out of it.

In the long term...

Address the practicalities Keep a regular bedtime routine. Don't let him drink too much in the hour before bed and take him to the toilet just before he goes to sleep. Make it easy for him to get to the loo by leaving his bedroom door open and the bathroom light on.

Talk to him See if you can discover any emotional causes of his bedwetting. Is he worried about something that could have triggered these episodes?

Seek advice While most children have grown out of bedwetting by the age of 6 or 7, if it happens a lot, keep a diary and see your GP to rule out any physical causes.

"Will bad people hurt us?"

As they get older, children are exposed to much more information about the world, and its risks. Your child may overhear older children or grown-ups talk about terrorist attacks, leading to anxiety that "bad people" may want to harm her and the people she loves, too.

SCENARIO | **After a terrorist attack, your child is worried about such events happening to her or anyone she knows.**

SHE SAYS

"Will bad people hurt us?"

YOU MIGHT THINK

"I don't know what to say to reassure her and stop her becoming anxious."

Children see the world in black and white terms – your child wants to believe that bad things only happen to bad people. So, it's shocking for her to discover that such events can happen to regular people. She will be picking up on anxious faces and take it to mean there's something to worry about.

Hearing about a terror attack in which innocent people have died has upset your child's in-built sense of fairness. While you may feel it is too soon to tackle such a big subject, you need to put this incident in perspective and let her know that she is going to be OK and so are the people she knows.

◆ SEE RELATED TOPICS ▶
I'm scared of the dark: pp.118–119
Will you die, too?: pp.166–167

CHILDREN TAKE THEIR CUE FROM YOU. RATIONALIZE YOUR OWN FEARS SO YOU CAN REASSURE YOUR CHILD.

HOW TO RESPOND

In the moment...

1

Listen to her Ask her what she knows and what she feels. By finding out what your child has heard and asking her to name her fears, it will help you to keep your answer simple and target her specific concerns.

2

Put it into context Tell her such attacks are rare and the reason they get so much attention is because they are unusual. Expect your child to keep asking the same questions until the threat in her mind has subsided. And repeat the same answer, calmly and consistently.

3

Give extra hugs Hug your child now and give more hugs than usual; focus on talking about the positives in life, which will reassure her the world is a safe place.

4

Help her feel she can protect herself Your child feels that her security is out of her hands. So, talk about the small ways she already keeps herself safe – using a seat belt in the car and wearing a helmet when she rides her bike, for example.

In the long term...

Limit exposure to on-screen news
Your child does not yet realize that every repeated news clip is not a new incident. It's best not to expose her to such images as she can't yet put them in context.

WHAT SHE'S THINKING

How do I know it won't happen to someone I love?

At this age, her world is split starkly into "good guys" or "bad guys". So, it's reassuring for her to discover that there are far more good guys working to keep her safe. In fact, making herself feel safe "right now" is top of her list of priorities, until she regains her previous balance of belief about safety in the world.

"It feels nice."

Children are curious and one of the first things that they want to learn about is their bodies. When they find their genitals, they discover touching these areas feels more pleasurable than other body parts, so some children may touch them repeatedly.

SCENARIO | **While watching a film together, you notice your child has one hand down his trousers.**

HE SAYS

"It feels nice."

Just as babies discover their fingers, toes, and belly buttons in their first year, they will also discover their genitals. As your child's hand coordination has improved, he may have got into a habit of enjoying these pleasurable feelings as a way of entertaining himself.

HOW YOU RESPOND TO SELF-TOUCHING CAN DECIDE WHETHER A CHILD GROWS UP FEELING PROUD OF OR SHAMEFUL ABOUT HIS BODY.

YOU MIGHT THINK

"I feel uncomfortable. What if he does it in front of others? He shouldn't be acting sexually at this age."

Even though it can make uncomfortable viewing, your child doesn't yet know what sex is, so self-touching isn't a sexual act but something he does to soothe himself. Be reassured that this behaviour is normal and will fade over time.

SEE RELATED TOPICS
I want a cuddle: pp.90–91
I'm scared of the dark: pp.118–119

HOW TO RESPOND

In the moment...

Help him find other ways to self-soothe Ask your child what else he can do to make himself feel good and explain that self-touching is a private activity. As he gets older and understands the line between public and private better, he will find other ways to comfort himself that are more socially acceptable.

Stay neutral Refrain from saying "Stop it" or "That's bad", which could make your child feel ashamed. If you make a fuss, he could do it more to get your attention.

Try distraction If your child's hands stray towards his genitals in public, keep a toy or book handy to give him instead. Or give him a security object – a blanket or a cuddly toy – to give him comfort.

In the long term...

Explain the science simply Talk about body changes. If your son ask why his penis becomes harder sometimes, you can talk about how the body reacts in other ways. For example, show him how the size of his pupils get bigger in dimmer light. Explain that both are reflexes.

Reframe your thinking The word masturbation is a term loaded with sexual overtones for many adults, which means you could pass on to your child that it's shameful. Instead, think of it as "self-pleasuring" or "self-exploration".

WHAT HE'S THINKING

"I don't understand what's so wrong about touching this part of my body. No one gets upset when I touch other bits."

Self-touching is a soothing activity, much like sucking a thumb; it's not sexual. Your child may touch himself more when he's bored, sleepy, or tense. He finds it distracting, pleasurable, and comforting. It has not yet become associated with private, sexual thoughts and feelings for him.

"Was that good?"

It's normal for children to crave their parents' approval. Over time, however, they also need to learn to develop their own intrinsic motivation to succeed so they want to achieve things for themselves, rather than only to please you.

SCENARIO | **In a game of tennis, your child hits the ball back twice in a row.**

" "

OVER TIME, CHILDREN DO BETTER IF THEY LEARN TO TAKE PRIDE IN THEIR OWN ACHIEVEMENTS.

SHE SAYS
___

"Was that good?"

Even before she could talk, your child learnt you were more likely to smile and respond warmly when she did things you wanted her to do, or did something well. This response also made her feel happier so she has learnt she wants to please you more. Your child also has a primal need for your approval because your love is the most important thing in the world to her.

◣ SEE RELATED TOPICS ▶
Do it myself: pp.38–39
Look what I've done!: pp.92–93

YOU MIGHT THINK

"If I praise her every time she does well, she will try harder, and she will excel."

You may feel you are being supportive by praising your child, and that if you praise her every time, she'll keep trying. Children do need praise to know when they've done well, but if you praise too much, she may become dependent on your approval.

WHAT SHE'S THINKING

"Mummy and Daddy look happier when I do well, so do they love me more?"

If you only lavish love and praise when your child does well, she may come to believe that your love is conditional on her successes. It's important she develops her own motivation to succeed.

HOW TO RESPOND

In the moment...

Focus on the process Praise her effort and perseverance along the way, rather than just the end result, such as winning or scoring.

Ask her how she feels While it's good that your child knows you're proud of her, it's just as important that she is proud of herself. Ask her if she is pleased with herself by prompting her. For example, say: "How does this make you feel?"

Don't limit approval While it's important not to praise your child too much, don't do the opposite by avoiding praising her completely.

In the long term

Be specific Instead of letting "well done" automatically roll off your tongue, be specific about what she has done well so she knows that you really notice what she does.

Don't encourage competitive behaviour Tell your child the best person to compete with is herself. That way she always wins, because with practice she will always get better at whatever she attempts.

"Will you die, too?"

When someone dies, young children usually don't yet understand that death is final: they think it's temporary or that their loved one has gone to sleep. So, it's useful to know how you can explain the situation sensitively while conveying the finality of this event.

SCENARIO | You have told your child his grandpa has died.

HE SAYS

"Will you die, too?"

YOU MIGHT THINK

"He doesn't need to know about death at his age."

A death in the family will trigger lots of questions. Your child might think: "Grandpa died in his sleep. Does that mean everyone can die in their sleep? What if that happens to Mummy and Daddy? Who will look after me?". Giving clear, open, and honest information will put his mind at rest.

Children can cope with knowing about death. But since your child thinks literally, it's crucial that you use words that convey the finality of death. Avoid phrases such as "gone to sleep" or "we've lost him". It's important that you don't confuse him or he may worry unnecessarily.

THOUGH YOUR INSTINCT MAY BE TO SHIELD YOUR CHILD, BEING OPEN IS BETTER THAN MAKING IT TABOO.

HOW TO RESPOND

In the moment...

(1)

Be open Explain that when someone is dead, their body does not move; they can't eat, talk, breathe, or feel pain and they don't wake up. Tell him everyone dies, but you don't expect it to happen to you for a long time.

(2)

Give a reason Explain simply why his grandpa died so he understands there's a reason his body stopped working: "Grandpa's heart got worn out because he lived for so long".

(3)

Relate it to life When explaining death to a child, it can help to link it to other experiences he knows, such as the death of a pet or a plant, so he understands it is final.

(4)

Ask him if he wants to draw his feelings Because children tend to put themselves at the centre of stories, they sometimes construct reasons why they might be to blame. In his mind, your child might imagine: "Grandpa died because I didn't do what I was told". Ask him if wants to talk about, draw, or role-play how he feels so you understand his thinking better.

In the long term...

Give it time Your child may want to talk about it for many months, so be prepared for more questions. Children also need tangible ways of mourning: going through family photos, making a keepsake box, releasing a balloon with his name on, or planting a tree can help.

WHAT HE'S THINKING

"Where's Grandpa now? Is he going to stop being dead so I can play with him again?"

Since your child may struggle with abstract concepts of time, such as "tomorrow" or "forever", it's hard for him to grasp that death is permanent and irreversible. But until he does, he will assume Grandpa is coming back. This limited understanding is also reflected in how he experiences grief. Children go through "islands of grief" — sad one minute, happy the next.

SEE RELATED TOPICS
I feel sad: pp. 132–133
Will bad people hurt us?: pp. 160–161

"You promised."

Parents are their child's entire universe at this age – they learn to trust the world by trusting their parents. This means that when you make a commitment it's important to stick to it, because children put so much faith in trusting that you will do what you say.

SCENARIO | **You said you would take your child to the park, but a work emergency means you can't now go.**

SHE SAYS

"You promised."

By now your child is learning the rules adults expect her to follow, including keeping your promises. Her sense of fairness means she expects you to do the same. If you break your promise, she may get the message your work is more important to you than she is.

SEE RELATED TOPICS

I love being with you: pp.108–109
You're always too busy: pp.128–129

YOU MIGHT THINK

"I meant to take her. How was I to know there'd be a work emergency on a Sunday?"

WHAT SHE'S THINKING

"Grown-ups let me down and don't do what they say."

It's not always possible to stick to every promise if circumstances change. The look of disappointment on your child's face can be hard to bear. But resist the temptation to mollify her; it may make you feel better but does more harm than good in the long term.

Children this age tend to think their parents make all the decisions, so it's tricky for your child to grasp that someone else (your manager) can tell you what to do. If she can see there is a good reason, and it was beyond your control, then the damage can be repaired.

HOW TO RESPOND

In the moment...

Say sorry Sympathize with your child's disappointment and give her an unconditional apology. Tell her how important she is to you. Explain that life is not perfect. Let her know you're disappointed, too.

Let your child choose a fun alternative for now Ask your child what she can do – colouring in a picture, say – while you finish work. Then, say as soon as you're finished you will do something special as planned.

In the long term...

Protect family time You can't foresee all eventualities, but do prioritize time with your child; put your phone away when you can and turn off your emails.

Don't overpromise Children have long and selective memories for things they particularly look forward to. Be careful about your wording and don't use the word "promise" lightly. Instead use phrases such as "I plan to…" or a "I am going to try" if there's any doubt at all.

Talk about your disappointments Managing disappointment is a difficult but important lesson for your child to learn. Talk about your own experiences to let her know how you coped and that the feeling passes.

Separation and divorce

Many families face the challenge of a separation or divorce. Whatever the reasons, it's difficult for everyone, and for children it can be especially frightening to see the two people they rely on go their separate ways.

Parents often like to assume that children are resilient. But parental divorce is a watershed event for children, especially if the life that follows is significantly different from the life that went before.

Being told that his parents no longer love each other, adjusting to going to and fro between different homes, and the sudden absence of one of the people who made him feel safe and loved, are all big challenges for your child to handle.

It's not always the split itself that causes the most damage, but the conflict and aggression between parents, so careful thought and handling can soften the impact on your child's wellbeing.

1
Tell him together
Most children will always remember being told about a separation. Present a united, optimistic front to make it a less painful memory.

4
Avoid buying treats out of guilt
Special treats can also make your child feel unsettled and as if he is being bribed to bury his sad feelings.

7
Be business-like
You must still act in the best interests of your child. By putting your feelings aside, you can team up to make better decisions.

9
Be patient
It can take at least two years for a child to settle back down emotionally after a split.

"" WHEN ADULTS RELATE TO EACH OTHER WELL AFTER A SEPARATION, CHILDREN BOUNCE BACK BETTER FROM ITS CHALLENGES.

GOOD PRACTICE

10 key principles

2
Set out the basics
Explain you aren't happy together and have agreed to live apart so you can stay friends and look after him without rows. Stress what will stay the same.

3
Reassure him
Explain what's happening to your child's life, not yours. Answer your child's principal worry, which will be: "Who's going to look after me?" Tell him you both will. The main difference is that you and your partner will be living in different places.

5
Avoid criticisms
Whatever has gone on between you both, your ex is still the only other parent your child has. Stay neutral in front of your child or the hostility can make them feel torn in two.

6
Listen to your child
Your child may feel many different emotions, including anger. She may also want you to stay together. Let her know now it's OK to feel sad. Allow her to talk about the situation from her perspective without taking sides or wanting to put forward your point of view.

8
Look after yourself
Take care of yourself so you can support your child. Ask family and friends for help, or try support groups. If there are issues to be resolved with your ex, mediation can help avoid hostility.

10
Keep up routines
Help normal life carry on as much as possible with play dates, trips, and family get-togethers, to help your child feel the world is still safe and predictable. Ask your partner to keep the same bedtimes and mealtimes at their home.

TAILORED ADVICE

Age by age

2–3
YEAR-OLDS

Give lots of comfort
Children often unload their feelings about big events by erupting over small triggers. Rather than see it as misbehaviour, give cuddles and reassurance.

Setbacks are normal
Children may regress – crying at bedtimes, wetting the bed, having separation anxiety. Be patient.

4–5
YEAR-OLDS

Tell the school
Let your child's teacher know so they can be understanding of any changes in behaviour.

A united front
Be polite and friendly to your ex so your child doesn't feel awkward about having you both at events such as school assemblies and concerts.

6–7
YEAR-OLDS

Not their fault
Children this age may blame themselves for the split because if they don't understand, they tend to fill in the gaps themselves. Be clear it wasn't his fault.

Being realistic
Your child may fantasize about reconciliation, but this can hold back recovery and make it harder for him to accept when you move on. Tell him this is an adult decision he can't influence.

"I want it to be perfect."

All parents want their children to try hard, whether it's with schoolwork, playing an instrument, mastering a sport, or any other skill. But sometimes it's children themselves who feel their best is never good enough.

SCENARIO | **When your child realizes she has written an "S" backwards in a birthday card, she rips it up.**

In moderate amounts, perfectionism can help a child try harder, but some can become so focused on getting everything right all the time, it can damage their self-belief and stop them trying new things. There are two main kinds of perfectionism:

● **Please-others perfectionism** is where your child wants others to think she never makes mistakes. Your child imagines others will laugh at her if she fails so she may become anxious and feel the need to get everything "just so" in an effort to stop others judging her negatively.

● **Please-yourself perfectionism** is where your child enjoys the feeling of pride she gets from meeting her own high standards, but can become so hooked on rewards, such as high test marks or praise from teachers, she may overload herself and put her other needs second.

See opposite to help you spot the signs of the different kinds of perfectionism and understand the triggers.

TELL YOUR CHILD EVERYONE MAKES MISTAKES AND THEY ARE OFTEN THE BEST WAY TO LEARN.

SEE RELATED TOPICS
I give up: pp.116–117
I'm useless: pp.210–211

THE ROUTE TO FOLLOW

Assessing perfectionism

PLEASE-OTHERS PERFECTIONISM

SIGNS

Overreacting to small mistakes and tearing up or scribbling on work if she feels it's not good enough.

Believing there's only one way to do a task.

Putting off doing homework or never giving it in at all.

Worrying a lot about what others think.

Stopping trying out of fear of failing.

TRIGGERS

Homework and classwork that is going to be assessed or compared.

Tests and exams.

Public performances, such as school concerts or assemblies.

RESPONSE

1. **Praise the effort** your child has put in, not the end result. Help her realize that enjoying and learning from an activity is more important than perfection.

2. **Tell your child** how the inner voice that says her work is "never good enough" is like a bully that ties up her thinking by making her feel sad and worried.

3. **Don't model perfectionist thinking** yourself. Set reasonable standards and don't continually stress the importance of performance.

4. **Explain there's a sliding scale** from one to ten for achievement, and it's never possible to get ten in everything. The middle is enough for most things.

5. **Foster a growth mindset** to help her move from "I can't" or "I will never" to "I will have a go".

PLEASE-YOURSELF PERFECTIONISM

SIGNS

Spending hours on schoolwork to make hers the best.

Wanting to join a lot of school clubs or play lots of instruments to show how multitalented she is.

Ignoring her own needs to have fun, play, and relax.

Comparing herself with others and bragging about her achievements to other children.

TRIGGERS

Sport matches she doesn't win.

Tests, projects, exams, and competitions in which she sets herself high targets or expects to beat everyone else.

Joint projects in which she has to work with others who don't have the same high standards.

RESPONSE

1. **Don't compliment** your child's work for being better than other children's. Celebrate its unique merits.

2. **Warmly acknowledge** your child's successes but don't go overboard as this will lead her to believe her self-worth is only tied to her achievement.

3. **Praise qualities** that can't be measured, such as kindness and humour.

4. **Instead of asking** what mark she got or how many goals she scored in a sports match, ask how much she learned from or enjoyed the work or game.

5. **Don't give love or rewards** conditional on her achievements, for example: "I'll buy you a new toy, if you get a good mark."

"No colouring on the wall."

Even though children are learning lots of rules at this age, it doesn't always mean they follow them every time. As they test boundaries and learn to control their impulses to stop themselves doing the first thing that comes into their heads, rules will be broken.

SCENARIO | **You catch your child drawing on the wall, as he repeats the rule he's breaking.**

HE SAYS

"No colouring on the wall."

YOU MIGHT THINK

"He's naughty. He knows he shouldn't draw on walls."

Your child wants to try out new things, but sometimes rules get broken. He may view this drawing as an "accident" when he held a crayon and then saw the wall – like a giant sheet of paper. Now you've reminded him it's wrong, he knows he will be in trouble and wants to tell you he knows better.

When you catch your child, he may confuse you by telling you he knew he wasn't supposed to do it. Such rule breaking is not defiance. Understand that he's conflicted – the areas of his brain that govern impulse and self-control are still being constructed, so his urge to create has overpowered his knowledge of the rules.

SEE RELATED TOPICS
I didn't do it: pp.142–143
Was that good?: pp.164–165

" "

JUST BECAUSE CHILDREN SAY THEY KNOW A RULE DOESN'T MEAN THEY CAN ALWAYS CONTROL THEIR BEHAVIOUR ENOUGH TO ABIDE BY IT.

WHAT HE'S THINKING

"I love the way I can move my crayon along the wall as I draw."

Your child is learning cause and effect — when he puts a crayon on a surface, a colourful line magically appears. At this developmental stage (with a level of hand–eye control), he finds it much easier and more enjoyable to scribble on a vertical surface.

HOW TO RESPOND

In the moment...

Understand his conflicting emotions If your child repeats back the rule when you catch him red-handed, don't be exasperated. Recognize that he does not yet have the understanding to explain why his impulses got the better of him.

Ask him to help remove it As a direct and immediate consequence, tell him to help clean off his drawing.

Explain what's appropriate Tell your child it's not OK to write on walls because walls don't just belong to him, and they are not meant to be drawn on. Teach him that "we don't write or draw on walls".

In the long term...

Provide other opportunities Help meet his need to draw on a larger scale by buying rolls of paper to use on a vertical easel or use outdoor chalk to make the most of big spaces outside.

Encourage his art sessions Drawing is one of the most important ways young children can express their thoughts and feelings, as well as developing motor skills. Hold back on showing your artistic talents, which may make your child frustrated because he will feel he cannot match them. Instead, be interested but let him decide what goes in his picture.

your 6—7 YEAR-OLD

"I have to tell you something!"

Children live almost completely in the present until they are about 7. They tend to interrupt adults when they are talking, because they are so focused on their own needs and they have not yet learned to fully control their impulses.

SCENARIO | You're on the phone to a friend and your child constantly interrupts you to tell you about a new game she's invented.

SHE SAYS

"I have to tell you something!"

YOU MIGHT THINK

"Why does she always interrupt? Can't I have any adult conversation?"

For the first few years of her life, you responded quickly to your child's cries and wants. Now, she is finding it hard to adjust to the idea that this isn't happening as much.

While you may be irritated by her nagging, you may also feel guilty about temporarily ignoring her, so consider if you're sending her mixed messages. But know, too, that if you do meet all her demands, it could give her the impression that only her needs matter.

" "

HELP YOUR CHILD UNDERSTAND THAT EVEN IF YOU ARE BUSY, YOU ARE ALWAYS INTERESTED IN HER.

WHAT SHE'S THINKING

"I can't wait. Mummy interrupts me when I'm busy. So, I can do it too."

By this age, children are learning to delay their gratification. Your child will be able to wait for short periods of time, with reassurance, but too long a wait can make her give up hope and feel rejected. It seems natural for her to interrupt you, since you've probably interrupted her playtime in the past.

SEE RELATED TOPICS
Carving out quality time: pp.84–85
I'm bored: pp.218–219

HOW TO RESPOND

In the moment...

Give her a signal Acknowledge that she is there – give her a smile and squeeze her hand to say that you've noticed she wants something. You could also put your fingers up to show how many minutes you expect to be.

Give a timeframe Your child has started to understand that time can be parcelled up into smaller packages in which to get things done. To avoid her thinking it will be ages until you come back to her, say: "I will need about 10 minutes of quiet time on the phone to Jane, and as soon as I'm finished I can listen to you."

In the long term...

Schedule calls for child-free times Time with your child is precious and children can take you being too busy to talk to them as rejection. As far as possible, plan long phone calls – or ask friends to call back – when your child is at school or in bed.

Plan ahead Prevention is the best way to head off interruptions. Prepare some toys, books, or other quiet activities for when you are on the phone. If the phone rings, ask your daughter: "Is there anything you need before I start talking? How will you keep yourself busy?".

Set a good example Adults often forget they interrupt children, too. Be polite and respectful if you want your child to do the same. For example, tell her: "It looks like you're having a great time playing that game. But I need to interrupt you in 2 minutes to tidy up before bedtime."

"It's not fair!"

As their sense of fairness develops, children may start to complain a lot if they feel they are being treated unjustly, especially compared with siblings. This behaviour marks the beginning of children starting to question their parents' decisions, as well as how the world works.

SCENARIO | **Your child asks why he has to go to bed an hour earlier than his 9-year-old sister.**

HE SAYS

"It's not fair!"

It's hard for your child to leave a situation when he feels like all sorts of exciting things could be happening in his absence. He may be over-reacting about having to go upstairs earlier because this is not really about bedtime, but more about how much time he spends with you.

YOU MIGHT THINK

"It's impossible. I can't win."

It's exasperating that, despite your best efforts, children will always look for the chance to accuse you of unfairness. That said, avoid countering with the remark: "Life isn't fair". While it may be true, save this for when your child is older. It's too big a concept for now.

BY GIVING HIM 'SPECIAL TIME' EACH DAY, HE IS LESS LIKELY TO CLAIM HE IS BEING UNFAIRLY TREATED AT OTHER TIMES.

WHAT HE'S THINKING

"I sometimes feel my parents don't love me the same as her."

Children this age are super-vigilant about getting the same amount of time, attention, perks, and treats as siblings; though, he might overlook the times when he gets the better deal. He may feel that his sister is your favourite and by staying up late he wants to show you that he's just as grown-up as her.

HOW TO RESPOND

In the moment...

Stop and listen Show you have registered his protest by saying: "I understand you're upset but there are good reasons why you go to bed earlier".

Give the reasons Different children have different needs at different ages. In the case of a 6-year-old and a 9-year-old, the younger child needs more sleep for his faster-growing brain to develop. Tell him that when he is 9, he will be allowed to stay up just as late.

Explain how "fair" is not always "identical" To illustrate that children need different things, give him another scenario. For example, if his sister likes books about hamsters and he doesn't, should they both get the same books for their birthdays?

Sidestep a debate Say your decision is final. Offer to take him to bed to read a story of his choice – so he feels he has got back some control over the situation – and say you will be happy to talk about bedtime rules tomorrow.

In the long term...

Give him special time If your child often says he's treated unfairly, it may be a symptom that he feels he's not getting enough of your attention. Ring-fence 10–15 minutes of one-on-one time with him each day, on top of bedtime story time. And include him in other household decisions, such as what to cook for dinner or where to go for a walk, so he feels his opinion is valued.

SEE RELATED TOPICS

But Mummy said I could: pp.186–187
But I'm not tired: pp.216–217

"I can't do it."

We all want our children to be confident, can-do learners, so it's worrying when your child's anxieties about her abilities make her feel it's not worth trying. She'll need your help to deal with these debilitating patterns of thought.

SCENARIO | **After barely starting her English homework, your child crumples up her worksheet and throws it on the floor.**

SHE SAYS

"I can't do it."

YOU MIGHT THINK

"I've always told her she's clever. How can I stop her being so negative?"

Your child feels anxious that she does not know what to write. This anxiety has triggered the fight-or-flight response in her brain, which means the rational part stops working and she really cannot work out how to tackle the task.

You may think your child is being overdramatic to try to get out of doing her work, or feel panicked that her lack of confidence will become a self-fulfilling prophecy. Your first instinct will likely be to tell to her she can do it, but she won't believe you because your words do not match her feelings.

WHEN YOUR CHILD SAYS SHE CAN'T DO SOMETHING, TELL HER SHE WILL GET BETTER WITH EFFORT.

WHAT SHE'S THINKING

"Because I think I can't do it, then it must be true. I'm just useless."

When your child thinks this thought, she believes she has to listen to it. She hasn't yet developed perspective and is prone to black and white thinking. Now she doesn't know how to start, she jumps to the conclusion that she can't do it.

SEE RELATED TOPICS
I'm useless: pp.210–211
I'm not as good as them: pp.220–221

HOW TO RESPOND

In the moment...

Tell her she can choose not to listen Negative self-talk is a form of internal bullying. Your child does not realize that when she hears these critical voices, she doesn't have to listen to them. Explain that telling herself she can't do something will only tie up her brain and stop it from working well.

Help her name these negative voices Encourage her to imagine the character in her head who tells her she can't do her work and give them a name, such as "Miss Can't" or "Miss Negative" so she can tell them to keep quiet.

Praise her for every step Let your child calm down. When she gives her homework another try, praise her for each step she makes. If she is really struggling, don't force her. Speak to her teacher to assess her capabilities and let them know she is showing signs of low confidence so they can help boost her belief in herself at school.

In the long term...

Give her a response Arm your child with short and to-the-point mantras that she can use to instantly counteract any negative thoughts that pop up, such as "the more I try, the more my brain grows".

Watch your criticism Sometimes parents can feel they have to coach their children through the increasingly competitive school system. However, comments you mean to be helpful can feel like criticism to children. To encourage your child, notice what she does right, rather than what she does wrong.

"I hate you!"

Children have more extremes of emotions than adults. So while your child adores you when he is happy, when things don't go his way he feels everything is terrible, including you. In that moment, he may interpret his frustration as hatred.

SCENARIO | **You won't let your child watch one more episode of his favourite TV programme.**

HE SAYS

"I hate you!"

YOU MIGHT THINK

"How could he say that? Does he mean it?"

Such words may be shocking to hear, but your child's outburst is also a sign that he trusts you to keep loving him, no matter what he says to you. It shows that he feels safe enough to express his anger and is confident you won't reject him.

When you love your child so much, it can be upsetting to hear him say something so cruel. While he is learning to express his emotions, it is important for you to maintain clear boundaries and not give in to what he wants, despite the intensity of the moment.

WHEN A CHILD SAYS 'I HATE YOU', HE IS TRYING TO PUT STRONG EMOTIONS HE DOES NOT KNOW HOW TO EXPRESS INTO SIMPLE WORDS.

WHAT HE'S THINKING

"I hate grown-ups being able to tell me what to do. It's not fair."

The words "I hate you!" spring from the emotionally reactive part of your child's brain, not the logical, thinking part – and thinking them is not the same as feeling them. He does not yet have the fluency or self-control to say: "I really like watching this and I am angry you won't let me watch as much as I want".

HOW TO RESPOND

In the moment...

Stay calm Your child is most likely to be too upset to hear anything you say. So, avoid responding with "Well, I love you" or "You know you love me, really", which will make your child feel ashamed. If you feel hurt, step away from the situation for a minute or two to stay in control of your feelings.

Name the emotions Your child is in a heightened emotional state, so name his feelings in short, clear sentences so he knows you understand he's upset, without justifying his behaviour. Say: "I can see you're angry that you can't watch another episode."

Explore ways of dealing with feelings When he feels frustrated or angry, suggest he takes some deep breaths or squeezes a toy as hard as possible. Although it will take time to master this, it is the start of your child learning to manage his emotions.

Focus on your child's frustration By reminding yourself his words are not personal and it's being given boundaries that he hates, not you, you will be able to keep calm.

In the long term...

Let the dust settle Don't punish your child. Afterwards, he might feel ashamed, so help him process this by explaining to him the difference between hating you and hating the rules, which mean that, for his own wellbeing, he can't always have what he wants.

SEE RELATED TOPICS
I wish I had a different family: pp.194–195
You never let me do anything: pp.238–239

"But Mummy said I could."

If you and your partner disagree on some of the basic rules in your family home, it can be frustrating at best and damaging at worst. It can create both distance and tension between a couple as well as confusion and insecurity for your child.

SCENARIO | **You come home to find your child on a tablet, despite the fact you agreed a rule of "no screens in the week".**

SHE SAYS

"But Mummy said I could."

Adults often come to parenthood with differing ideas about how children should be brought up. As a result, conflict over how to parent – especially, sticking to the rules – can cause tension. Working together, though, will help your child understand what is expected of her and, in turn, make her feel more secure.

SEE RELATED TOPICS
It's not fair!: pp.180–181
Stop fighting: pp.214–215

YOU MIGHT THINK

"I always ensure she has no screens in the week. Why is my partner making my job harder?"

WHAT SHE'S THINKING

"Mummy and Daddy can't agree on the rules. What should I do?"

Agreeing and setting rules that children stick to is hard work, so you're likely to resent your partner if you feel they've undermined your efforts. You may also feel angry that your authority is being questioned in front of your child, and now she has spotted how to play you off against one another.

Although your child doesn't yet have the cognitive capacity to understand why, she may be scared, confused, and angry when caught between parents. Even if she wins a short-term gain, she would feel safer and more cared for if both of you were on the same page.

HOW TO RESPOND

In the moment...

Hold your tongue Avoid showing your anger or disapproval of the situation in front of your child, as it undermines the authority of both parents.

Reaffirm the situation When your child says "But Mummy lets me do that," reply calmly "Sometimes we can do things a bit differently but we've goth agreed that you need to finish off on the tablet now." Restate the rule to your child so she knows to stick to it.

In the long term...

Put on a united front At other times when you disagree with the way your partner handles a situation ask: "Can I help?" instead of objecting to what you see as them doing wrong in front of your child.

Agree a team approach Later on sit down with your partner and talk through your general values about child-rearing. Explain to each other why yours are important to you and then find a mutually agreed middle ground.

Don't "compensate" If you have a tendency to be the stricter parent and feel your partner is being particularly laissez faire, don't become even stricter as a result.

Good manners

A baby's burps and yawns seem adorable. But not long after toddlers start to walk and talk, they are quickly expected to start behaving as mini-adults and learn the grown-up rules of social behaviour.

Most parents are keen to teach their children manners. But, good manners are more than niceties of learning to use a knife and fork properly, they are also about developing an awareness of the needs and feelings of others – and treating them with respect.

Research has also found that good manners are an important and life-long skill for making friends and enjoying professional success throughout life.

Children can start to learn manners from the age of 2 as they begin to develop an understanding of the social world and to comprehend that others have feelings, too, and also need to be treated with courtesy. At times, you will have to use your judgment to ensure expectations of your child's behaviour are in line with what he is capable of developmentally. Consistency, repetition, and patience will be key.

1

Make a commitment
You will need to make a conscious decision to bring up a well-mannered child because you will need to consistently demonstrate good manners yourself, both in and out of the home.

4

Have family meals
The best place to teach manners is at family mealtimes where eventually, like grown-ups, children will sit at the table, use their cutlery, use their indoor voice, not make noises when they eat, chew with their mouth closed, and wait until the end of the meal to leave the table.

6

Make it fun
Show how saying "magic" words such as "please" and "thank you" will mean they are more likely to have their requests met.

GOOD PRACTICE

8 key principles

2
Start simply
Prompting your child to say "please" and "thank you" is the easiest way to start. As soon as these become second nature to him, focus on adding one or two more at a time so he can completely master those before adding more.

3
Encourage eye contact
Children are often judged by adults and seen as more friendly by their peers at school if they use eye contact. To help your child practise, make it a game: ask your child to find out the colour of the eyes of the people he speaks to.

5
Explain why manners are important
Courtesy is about treating others well and being treated well in return. Talk about how good manners can make life easier and more enjoyable. Others will like them more and be kinder to them, too.

7
Compliment them
Let them overhear you praise their good manners to others and enjoy the positive attention they get when you point out their courteous behaviour.

8
Explain that good manners = friendship skills
Greeting people, facing towards them, and waiting for their turn to talk are also important for getting along with others and making friends.

TAILORED ADVICE

Age by age

2–3
YEAR-OLDS

Daily greetings
Say "Good morning" to your child every day and greet other family members too.

Toy helpers
Use stuffed animals, dolls, or puppets to play mealtimes and practise saying: "Please", "Thank you", "You're welcome", and "Excuse me".

4–5
YEAR-OLDS

A personal note
Now children are starting to learn to write and draw, get them to draw or sign their name on thank-you notes, and tell them how happy this makes others feel.

Board games lessons
Playing board games gives children the chance to learn cooperation and turn-taking while having fun.

6–7
YEAR-OLDS

The host with the most
Before a play date, talk about greeting guests at the door, asking what they'd like to do, sharing toys, and saying goodbye afterwards.

Manners and feelings
Point out how holding a door or giving up a seat for an older person recognizes their presence and needs – and makes them appreciative and happy.

"No one likes me."

Having good friends is becoming increasingly important to children at this age. They have now gone beyond playmates to wanting to form stronger bonds with others who share their interests. But if a child gets left out, she will feel hurt.

SCENARIO | **Your child has come out of school and told you she has no friends.**

SHE SAYS

"No one likes me."

It's not unusual for kids to say they have no friends from time to time. At this age, children are black and white thinkers, so a refusal to play one day may be taken as general dislike. Some need help interpreting social cues from others to know how to join in, take turns, and be a fun playmate.

" "

EVERY CHILD WILL FEEL FRIENDLESS AT SOME POINT. YOUR ROLE IS TO OFFER PERSPECTIVE AND HELP YOUR CHILD FEEL LOVED AT HOME.

YOU MIGHT THINK

"I feel so helpless. I can't make friends for her."

It's heartbreaking to think of your child alone in a playground, unable to find a friend to play with. You may need to give her guidance and support on where she may be going wrong, as research has pointed out that children often don't know unless it is pointed out to them.

SEE RELATED TOPICS
They're being mean to me: pp.192–193
I'm not playing any more: pp.224–225

WHAT SHE'S THINKING

"I had no one to play with today. Will anyone like me again?"

Your child is discovering that friendships have ups and downs – but just because she felt lonely today doesn't mean there won't be playmates tomorrow. If she feels rejected at school, it's even more vital that she feels accepted at home.

HOW TO RESPOND

In the moment...

Listen and give her a cuddle Acknowledge her feelings and let her know she is loved. Reassure her that friendships change fast and it's always possible to build new friendship skills.

In the long term...

Practise friend-making skills Children can learn "social smarts", which improve with practice. Help her learn by playing board games (taking turns) and train her how to connect with others (look people in the eye and smile).

Talk about resolution skills If your child is having a lot of rows with her friends, then offer some strategies to get through her "friendship rough spots". Help her to learn how to both accept and give an apology when there is a falling out.

Help her learn empathy If she can learn to better understand how others feel, she can learn to respond with the right words and gestures, and will be accepted more. Give her practice by playing a game of watching other children's faces in the playground or on TV and trying to guess their feelings.

Encourage a wide friendship circle Schools are social pressure cookers. Not having as many friends as she'd like in her year group won't matter as much to her if she has other friends outside school.

"They're being mean to me."

It's upsetting when your child tells you that others have been mean to him. It's also natural to want to protect your child from hurt. But, as children learn to socialize, they need to learn to cope with a degree of "normal" social pain.

SCENARIO | **Your child tells you that other boys wouldn't let him join in their game at break-time.**

HE SAYS

"They're being mean to me."

YOU MIGHT THINK

"My child is being bullied. I have to do something."

It's not unusual for children to sometimes say they have no friends. At this age, your child is sensitive because he is forming his identity based on what his peers think of him. But if he says this a lot, it may be a sign he needs practice interpreting social cues and working out how to join in games.

Though you may feel protective, it doesn't help to label every act of meanness as bullying – usually a long-term, organized campaign by a more powerful child against a socially weaker one to cause hurt. If you see any deliberate and persistent targeting, you'll need to step in to help.

SEE RELATED TOPICS

I don't want to go to school: pp.196–197
But all my friends have one: pp.208–209

66 99

AS A PARENT, YOUR JOB IS TO TRAIN HIM TO DEAL WITH FRIENDSHIP ISSUES HIMSELF.

WHAT HE'S THINKING

"It's not fair they're being mean to me. Does that mean I'll never have any friends?"

Friendships are fundamental for a child's emotional wellbeing and self-confidence. At this age, children are all-or-nothing thinkers. So, if, for instance, your child's friend told him he didn't want to play with him that day, he may take it as a general sign he is not likeable, unless told otherwise by you.

HOW TO RESPOND

In the moment...

①

Discover the details See if you can tease out the details. Ask him to tell you what a camera would have seen if it had filmed the interaction. You could also role-play with toys so you understand the dynamics.

②

Explain it can change tomorrow Children's friendships change fast at this age. Say to your child that just because someone was mean to him today doesn't mean he won't have fun in the playground tomorrow.

③

Help him not to take it heart When others are being mean, don't allow your child to blame himself or think it means he is unlikeable. Remind him of his qualities.

④

Be objective Separate past memories from your child's present hurts; if you over-react, the incident could be blown out of proportion. Your child needs to understand that conflict is an inevitable part of relationships.

In the long term...

Support him at home Help build your child's self-worth by making it clear you like him and want to spend time with him. Mean remarks from others will never cut as deep if your child has a strong inner core.

"I wish I had a different family."

As a parent, you've done your best to establish a loving home, so when your child is angry with you, it's upsetting to hear her say she wishes she had a different family. Identifying the feelings underneath can help you respond calmly.

SCENARIO | **You tell your child she can't go to a classmate's party because there's a family occasion you all have to attend.**

SHE SAYS

"I wish I had a different family."

YOU MIGHT THINK

"How could she say such a hurtful thing when we've only tried to do the best for her?"

As your child spends more time outside the home, she realizes other families have different rules, so will compare yours with theirs. She now also understands your feelings can be hurt. As she has lost her temper she is prepared to say something shocking, in the moment, to change your mind.

You may be upset because your child's remark feels like a rejection of the home you've created, your values, and your family unit. Her comment might also bring up guilt about past parenting mistakes, or your present situation, if it's not as happy as you'd like.

SEE RELATED TOPICS
But Mummy said I could: pp.186–187
You never let me do anything: pp.238–239

WHAT SHE'S THINKING

"I really want to go to the party. A different family would let me."

Your child is using "selective attention" to look for evidence that confirms her view: that if she was in different family, she would be able to go to the party. But what she really means is that you don't understand how much she wants to go.

HOW TO RESPOND

In the moment...

①

Don't take it personally This is mostly about her tangled feelings. Your child is dealing with her difficult emotions by projecting them onto you. Maintain your rational thinking by remembering that, as the person who loves her unconditionally, you are the safest target for her frustration.

②

Acknowledge what's underneath Try not to get triggered and instead put into words why it sounds like she is frustrated so she knows you understand. When she has calmed down, tell her that while it's fine to feel angry, this isn't a reason to be unkind.

③

Talk through your reasons When the more logical part of her brain has regained control, explain that although parties are fun, family events are usually more important. She is a key part of the family and she would be missed.

In the long term...

See her perspective While your child may be lashing out, ask yourself if there's anything happening that could make her feel like an outsider, such as sibling conflict. Could this be a plea for one-on-one time?

Pull closer Plan activities that bring you together so your child feels a sense of belonging. Eat dinner as a family and instil family rituals, such as a weekly film night.

"I don't want to go to school."

All children have the odd day when they don't feel like going to school. But, apart from illness, there can be other reasons they want to stay at home. If it happens repeatedly over a few weeks, work out what's worrying your child and why he doesn't want to go.

SCENARIO | **Your child refuses to get dressed in the morning and go to school.**

HE SAYS

"I don't want to go to school."

YOU MIGHT THINK

"He's just playing up. He's got to go to school. And I've got work."

If your child has no symptoms of illness, there must be something else behind his refusal. Consider his character – is he normally a get up and go child or has he always been a reluctant pupil? Is there an underlying issue? All types of upset create anxiety that can cause him to want to stay at home.

It's easy to go into a panic as you will have many conflicting feelings. Is he really ill? Is he manipulating you? How strict should you be? If you work, you are likely to be worried about having to take the day off – and resentful if you suspect your child is not actually ill.

SEE RELATED TOPICS
No one likes me: pp.190–191
Why do you have to go to work?: pp.236–237

" **"**

BE POSITIVE ABOUT SCHOOL. EXPLAIN HE'LL LEARN LOTS OF SKILLS HE NEEDS TO KNOW TO GROW UP.

WHAT HE'S THINKING

"Home feels safe and calm to me."

Children's bodies are sensitive to emotions, If your child is feeling anxious about something, he'll want the security of being at home with a parent. In fact, he could be so worried – about a test at school or a friendship issue – that he can work himself into having a real tummy ache.

HOW TO RESPOND

In the moment...

Hold the line Be patient with him and reflect back his emotions so he knows you are listening, but at the same time be firm and don't cave in.

Take your time If you are becoming stressed, call ahead to school and explain that your child may be in late; and, if necessary, let work know, so that you can stay calm and address the situation thoroughly.

In the long term...

Make mornings manageable Break down getting ready for school into small, easily achievable steps. Give lots of praise for each step your child completes – getting up, getting dressed, eating breakfast, and arriving in the school playground.

Help him express himself "Externalizing" is a way of getting children to name their worries. Ask your child to create a character who says the things that make him anxious. The next time your child hears these worries, ask if his "worry gremlin" is talking loudly or ask what it's saying. This way you can work with him to "fight back" against the emotions.

Speak to your child's teacher and GP If there's a pattern emerging, work with the school to identify the problem. It's worth taking your child to the doctor to rule out any physical issues if he often mentions tummy aches and headaches.

"She's my best friend."

When children first go to nursery school, they are usually happy to play alongside whoever is nearby. However, by 6 or 7 your child may be seeking out one special "best" friend who they click with and whose company they prefer over other people's.

SCENARIO | Your child has told you that she now has a "best friend".

SHE SAYS

"She's my best friend."

YOU MIGHT THINK

"Is she forming an exclusive bond too soon?"

Having a special friend to pair up with at school can make children feel safer. Because she fears being left out, your child will be happy to always have the security of someone who'll want to be her partner. She will also feel proud that someone likes her enough to appoint her as their best friend

If both children have found a connection and like each other equally, such friendship will be a source of great joy and fun. That said, don't worry if she doesn't have a best friend. From now, you'll see her working out where she fits in as she seeks out friends to share her inner thoughts with.

> **GOOD FRIENDSHIPS WILL HELP YOUR CHILD FEEL HAPPIER AT SCHOOL, BUT NOT EVERY CHILD HAS TO HAVE A 'BEST FRIEND'.**

WHAT SHE'S THINKING

"I want her to play just with me."

The flip-side of best friendship is that it can come with strings attached. As children's social relationships become more complex, they may promise best friendship as long as certain conditions are met or take the title away if the best friend plays with others. They may also change best friends daily.

HOW TO RESPOND

In the moment...

Put the relationship in context If your child tells you she has a best friend, welcome the news and let her introduce the friend.

Remind her of other friends Do take the opportunity to talk about all her other friends. And prompt her on including others in games, so that this best friendship does not become exclusive and so she does not feel alone when it inevitably hits a sticky patch.

In the long term...

Get her to use other terms as well Children can also describe others they are in a trusting relationship with as "good" or "close" friends. Explain that if she gives one the title "best friend", she will give the impression others are less important to her.

Don't see it as the ideal Best friends can offer security in always having a partner, but not being tied to one person can also offer freedom. As long as your child is happy, it's fine if she has a best friend – and fine if she doesn't. Help her to comprehend this, too.

Be prepared for ups and downs Research has found that if she has got a best friend then it's that person she will have the most arguments with. So, do be ready to support her through such situations. That said, because of their close relationship, they will also be more invested in making up afterwards.

SEE RELATED TOPICS
They're being mean to me: pp.192–193
I've got a boyfriend: pp.222–223

School pressure

Even in primary school children start to be prepared for standardized tests in certain subjects – and it will become evident that some children find the work easier than others.

It's common to fret about how your child performs at school. Yet it's important to keep this in perspective, and remember that schools measure only a limited range of a child's abilities.

A resilient child

Wherever your child sits in the spectrum of academic performance, build resilience by helping him feel competent in lots of other areas of life, especially those that can't be measured in a classroom – qualities such as kindness, generosity, or creativity.

Even if you have a child who scores well in school tests, reinforce the fact that you don't expect them to get top marks every time and that they can only do their best.

Do make it clear that your love for your child is unconditional – she never has to "earn" it with good marks.

" "

REMEMBER THAT EMOTIONAL WELLBEING IS THE BEST PREDICTOR OF FUTURE HAPPINESS AND SUCCESS, NOT TEST SCORES.

1

Value every quality
Encourage children to see themselves as well-rounded characters who are more than the sum of their achievements on paper. Recognize and praise qualities, such as humour, gratitude, social skills, self-control, optimism, and grit.

4

Celebrate uniqueness
Rather than compare your child with others, acknowledge the combination of qualities that makes your child uniquely who they are.

6

Praise effort
Instead of praising your child for a fixed skill, such as being "good at maths", praise them for the qualities they have control over, such as persistence and effort. Explain they can always get better at a subject.

GOOD PRACTICE

8 key principles

2
Use the word "yet"
If a child can't do something easily, it's usually because they haven't had the chance to learn or practise how to do it. Acknowledge that learning is on-going and they will get better at any task with practice.

3
Create a haven at home
Aim to make your home a place where your children can retreat from the world and recharge from the school day. Just as important as schoolwork is downtime, fresh air, exercise, and family activities.

5
Compete for their personal best
Explain there is just one person who is truly worth beating – themselves. This way children can always feel a sense of achievement when they improve.

7
Make time for play
Play and learning are not two different things. Studies show that science and maths are best learned through real life and experience. Children will understand money, for example, if they are taught to use it, and science if they spend more time in nature so they can see how key concepts work in the real world.

8
Explain how her brain works
Help your child understand that the brain is like a muscle that keeps getting stronger through exercise. Older children may comprehend how neural pathways are built by practice and repetition and how electrical signals make connections between the nerve cells to form a network. The more those cells are linked, the stronger the network becomes, forming a memory and eventually a skill.

❗
TAILORED ADVICE
Age by age

2–3
YEAR-OLDS

Free play Even very young children spot when adults try to take control of their games and "teach" them something, so don't turn play into a lesson.

Simple is best Don't fall for claims on high-tech toys or apps implying they can make your child smarter. Children learn best from the simplest toys.

4–5
YEAR-OLDS

Competitive parenting Avoid competing with other parents over reading and maths levels. Turning these skills into a race can be stressful for your child.

Natural talents Help children build on the activities they are naturally drawn to, so they also feel competent in other areas.

6–7
YEAR-OLDS

Actively interested Even though your child may be starting to be tested at school now, ask him about what he's learning about, not what grade he got.

Hold back Children often hear parent's comments on homework, even if meant constructively, as criticism. Point out more of what they are doing right than what they're doing wrong.

"Homework is boring."

Many children get set a certain amount of homework as soon as they start primary school. But when a child comes home after a day of lessons, often the last thing they want to do is sit down and do more school work. So, many children will make excuses to avoid it.

SCENARIO | **Your child refuses to sit down to complete her maths worksheet.**

SHE SAYS

"Homework is boring."

YOU MIGHT THINK

"Why do we have to have this battle again? I've had a long day."

Clarify what your child means when she says homework is boring. Does she mean it's not as fun as playing or that she's not sure how to do it? Once you've listened, understood, and helped her look at the task, she's more likely to get down to it.

Your child is learning the skills and self-discipline she needs to do homework. Don't get angry with her repeated refusals. It's tempting to help her do it but that would send the wrong message: if she makes enough fuss you'll do it. Your role is to give her good habits and show her how to take responsibility.

WITH A GOOD ROUTINE, HOMEWORK WILL IMPROVE ALL BY ITSELF AND YOUR CHILD WILL BE MORE RECEPTIVE TO GETTING DOWN TO IT.

WHAT SHE'S THINKING

"This looks hard. I want homework to go away."

At this developmental stage, she only has a short attention span and definitely won't want to do homework as soon as she gets home. What's more, her maths lesson was hours ago and she may worry she won't be able to apply what was taught in the lesson on her own.

◀ SEE RELATED TOPICS ▶

I'm useless: pp.210–211
Do I have to do music practice?: pp.230–231

HOW TO RESPOND

In the moment...

Don't stress At your child's age, learning through play is just as important as ploughing through a maths worksheet. As long as she's doing a little bit of reading or mental arithmetic each day, it's enough.

Keep sessions short and doable Most teachers will tell parents how much time they want pupils to spend on their homework, so stick to that. A visual device, such as an egg-timer, can show her when the homework session is over. Sit nearby – with your own "homework" – so you can offer encouragement and be called upon to answer questions.

In the long term...

Reward her afterwards When your child completes homework without any complaints, immediately offer her a game with you or set up a rewards jar. Put a pebble or marble in every time she does homework without complaint and agree a small treat when she gets to five.

Set up a homework base Create a place to do all homework. The kitchen table is probably the best place so you can be close. Clear away anydistractions, such as devices and toys, and equip it with all she needs – pencils, rubbers, and rulers.

Choose the same time The hour you set may vary, depending on your child's after-school activities, but agree a set time for homework for each day of the week and stick to it. When it becomes a routine, it becomes a fact of life and there are fewer rows.

"I'm the best."

As the approval of peers becomes more important, children sometimes think others will like them more if they say they are particularly good at something. However, they may not yet realize that "boasting" can be annoying.

SCENARIO | **Your child keeps telling other kids he is the best goal scorer in football.**

HE SAYS

"I'm the best."

Children are now becoming aware of how they are different. As your child starts to define himself as a person, he compares his achievements, skills, and possessions with others. He may believe that if other children are impressed by him, they will want to be his friend.

HELP CHILDREN KNOW THAT THEY DON'T HAVE TO COMPARE THEIR ACHIEVEMENTS WITH OTHERS TO FEEL GOOD.

SEE RELATED TOPICS
They're being mean to me: pp.192–193
I'm not as good as them: pp.220–221

YOU MIGHT THINK

"Other children won't like him if he keeps showing off."

It's good that your child takes pride and has confidence in his abilities. As any proud parent, you want to give him due praise, but you may be tempted to ask him to pipe down about his skills, since no one likes a show-off. Talk about how giving compliments to others makes them feel good, too.

WHAT HE'S THINKING

"But if I'm good at something, why can't I say so?"

Your child may not understand that boasting does not draw others to him. He does not yet realize that celebrating his successes can make others feel as if they are falling short. He may need help in understanding how friends feel when he keeps reminding them he is the best.

HOW TO RESPOND

In the moment...

Talk about skills Explain that everyone has a special skill and friends don't necessarily have the same strengths. Tell your child while he may be good at football his friend may be very good at maths or drawing.

Discuss friendship Tell him that friendship is about enjoying other people's company, not proving to them how amazing you are. To connect with other children, show him how to look for what he has in common with others, not what sets him apart.

In the long term...

Show him unconditional love At school, your child may also be noticing how children are ranked and given prizes. So, he may not want to feel left out. Make sure he gets plenty of unconditional love at home.

Be fair in your praise Research has found parents who often tell their children they are more "special" than others can give them an inflated self-image. Focus on giving warmth and love, whatever his accomplishments.

Encourage skills at home Let him know you are proud of his efforts, and that while it's fine to talk about his achievements in detail at home with family members, it might be better if he summarized them for his friends.

"You're embarrassing me."

In the early years, your child probably told you were the kindest and bravest Mummy in the world or the funniest and most generous Daddy. So, it can come as a shock the first time your child says you act in a way that is embarrassing to them.

SCENARIO | **Your child has said she does not want you to kiss her goodbye in the school playground any more.**

SHE SAYS

"You're embarrassing me."

YOU MIGHT THINK

"I'm sad she no longer wants me to kiss her in public."

As social awareness increases around this age, your child is noticing how her home and family are different from those of other people. She also sees that other children are spotting these differences and will sometimes talk about them.

You are likely to feel hurt that the golden period when your child thought you could do no wrong has come to an end. Yet she's just feeling peer pressure. While you may understand why she says it's embarrassing when you kiss her goodbye, don't take it personally.

SEE RELATED TOPICS
No one likes me: pp.190–191
You never let me do anything: pp.238–239

HOW TO RESPOND

In the moment...

Don't be angry Avoid taking it personally. Your child doesn't mean to be hurtful. She believes she's protecting you from other children's judgment and comments.

Respect the requests – within reason Now your child is becoming more self-conscious, adapt to reasonable requests – treating her in a more grown-up way in front of others – that are a necessary part of development. It's a sign she is becoming her own person.

In the long term...

Remember your own childhood You probably thought your parents were embarrassing when you were a child – but now you're grown-up, you love the qualities that make them different. Use humour to tell her how you once felt the same at her age.

Ask your child to think about how you feel As part of training your child how to think about the feelings of others, use "I feel" statements to explain how you felt when she told you that you were embarrassing.

Offer some input To be sensitive to your child, you could ask her when she's happy for you to give her kisses and cuddles outside the home and when she'd rather you held back. Do let her know that it's important not always to give in to peer pressure.

WHAT SHE'S THINKING

"My friends don't get goodbye kisses. I don't want them either."

Just as your child wants to fit in with her peers, she wants you to fit in — and that means not standing out from other parents. It's not that she doesn't like you (or won't want kisses at home), she's anxious of other children passing comment on it.

FINDING YOUR PARENTS EMBARRASSING IS A NATURAL PART OF THE JOURNEY TOWARDS ADOLESCENCE.

"But all my friends have one."

As children become more aware of their place among peers, they learn that fitting in makes them feel happy. And to fit in, they may say that they "need" new gadgets, toys, or clothes. How you respond is a chance to put possessions into perspective.

SCENARIO | **Your child has asked for his own tablet so he can play the latest video games.**

HE SAYS

"But all my friends have one."

Your child is now exposed to more media and programmes with adverts, many of which are aimed directly at him to encourage "pester power". As he starts to compare himself to others, he is affected by a powerful new force – fear of missing out. He wants what he thinks his friends have to feel "normal".

YOU MIGHT THINK

"Maybe I should get him one, or he'll get left out. I work hard to be able to buy him things."

Adults can't escape peer pressure, either. You may feel you're not a good parent if you don't buy him one. You may remember wanting the latest toy as a child, and now you want to meet that need for him. Guilt may surface, too, if you feel you're not spending enough time with him.

SEE RELATED TOPICS
No one likes me: pp.190–191
I'm not as good as them: pp.220–221

WHAT HE'S THINKING

"I really, really need it. My friends will want to play with me more if I do."

Because children of his age are also forming social hierarchies, he may unconsciously believe that this must-have gadget will give him status within his social group. He does not yet have the life experience to understand that it's his personal qualities that matter, not what he owns.

HOW TO RESPOND

In the moment...

①

Ask why he wants it Get a sense of why he feels he needs this gadget so badly. Talk about the difference between "needs" and "wants".

②

Put his request into perspective Do all his friends really have one, as he claims? By talking to other parents, you may find out that's not actually the case.

③

Facilitate his wants within limits If you simply give your child the tablet straightaway, he may take it for granted that he will always get what he wants. Instead ask if he would like to put his request on a "waiting list" to see if he wants it as much in a few weeks' time or suggest he hangs on until his birthday or Christmas.

④

Help him value the personal Explain that it's never possible to buy friends and the real reason other children want to spend time with him is because he's fun to be with, cooperates, and is fair in games, for example, not because he has the latest gadgets.

In the long term...

Stand up to peer pressure If your child talks about what his friends' parents allow, use the phrase "in our family" to help him understand that different families have different values and priorities.

"I'm useless."

At this age, parents want children to start to take responsibility for their actions. But when they make mistakes, some children may wrongly use them as evidence that they are "useless" or "not good enough"; these feelings of shame can be the start of negative self-talk.

SCENARIO | Your child knocks your favourite mug off the table and breaks it.

SHE SAYS

"I'm useless."

Your child is now forming a sense of who she is compared with others. As well as judging others, she is judging herself. She feels guilty and worried you will be upset. Rather than see this accident as an understandable mistake, she is using catastrophic thinking to tell herself she never does anything right.

SEE RELATED TOPICS
I can't do it: pp.182–183
I'm not pretty enough: pp.242–243

YOU MIGHT THINK

"If she feels really bad about it, maybe she'll be more careful next time."

If the mug was precious, anger at your child's carelessness may allow your emotional brain to take over and to tell her how thoughtless she's been, making your child feel worse. Such shaming is often used by adults in the mistaken belief it's the best way to get through to them.

MAKING MISTAKES IS A NORMAL PART OF GROWING UP. HELP YOUR CHILD TO LEARN FROM THEM IN A CONSTRUCTIVE, SHAME-FREE WAY.

WHAT SHE'S THINKING

"I'm such an idiot. I always will be."

Instead of thinking "I did something stupid", your child is thinking "I am stupid". Shame is a painful emotion, and children are particularly vulnerable because whether they show it or not, they want to please their parents. And if they don't live up to expectations, they feel they are failing.

HOW TO RESPOND

In the moment...

Say "it's OK" and listen Rather than focus on the broken mug, hear what your child has to say in her own words. Explain that mistakes are a part of life.

Tell her to be kind to herself The opposite of shame is compassion. Point out that she would not let friends say such things to themselves. So, why is she doing that?

Don't use shaming Using shame to discipline children has been found to increase levels of the stress hormone cortisol, which is damaging to a child's developing brain.

In the long term...

Help her to identify self-critical voices Saying she can't do anything right is a sign that negative thoughts about herself are pushing out positive ones – and that she feels unable to change. Explain she can argue with those thoughts, silence them, or replace them with kinder ones about her strengths and achievements.

Check for perfectionism Children who are especially hard on themselves may also have a particularly harsh inner critic that tells them they must be perfect. Talk to her about her expectations of herself as well as explaining that perfection is never possible. Perfectionism tends to run in families. Explore your ideas around perfectionism so that you can model a healthy approach to success and failure.

Money matters

To a child, money is a commodity that allows grown-ups to go into shops and take whatever they want. It takes many stages of development to understand what money is, but there's plenty you can do to guide them.

Although many parents may think children don't yet need to know about the economic realities of life, research has found that it's better to get children into good money habits when they are young – in fact, attitudes to saving and spending are set by the age of 7.

Giving pocket money also plays an important part in teaching children mental arithmetic. What's more, having to deal with regular amounts of money is one of the best ways to train children how to control their impulses, learn patience, have willpower, and delay gratification. When children find that saving up their pocket money for something they really want feels better than simply splurging it all in one go on frivolous stuff, it's a milestone in their self-regulation. Plus, practising how to save now will set them up with sensible money habits for life.

❝ ❞

SHOPPING WITH YOUR CHILD AND TALKING THROUGH SPENDING DECISIONS IS TRAINING FOR THE FUTURE.

1
Teach them the basics
Until the age of 5, children view coins as toys. To increase understanding, play shops and talk about how differently valued coins look different.

4
Teach them where money comes from
Unless told otherwise, young children think money is free and banks and cash machines give it out to anyone. Help them understand that money is earned by going to work.

6
Explain finite finances
Young children find it hard to grasp that money can only be spent once. Give them £1 to go shopping to see that once it's gone, it's gone.

9
Peg pocket money to age
Children understand money enough to get regular pocket money at about the age of 6. A simple rule of thumb, for future, is to give them an amount equal to half their age.

Age by age

2–3
YEAR-OLDS

Play money
Show children how money can be exchanged for goods by playing shops and cafés with them.

Size is everything
Children at this age believe that one coin can buy anything. Point out how different coins and notes can buy items of different value.

4–5
YEAR-OLDS

Universal cash
Children believe that everyone has money, given to them for free by banks or by shopkeepers. Explain how money is earned.

Get real
Letting children touch and feel money and pay in shops is one of the best way to teach them what money means in concrete terms.

6–7
YEAR-OLDS

Ready and waiting
Now children can count and understand how money works, it's time for you to start regular pocket money.

The saving habit
Teach them that saving is a good thing and praise them for their self-control when they save up their cash. Help them see the amount grow in a glass jar.

GOOD PRACTICE

12 key principles

2
Give them practice
Even in a cashless society, your child needs to handle coins and notes to learn what money is. Let him have practice paying so he sees buying is a transaction.

3
Get them into saving
Research shows that children who are encouraged to save are far more likely to continue saving as adults. Put pocket money in two jars: one for spending and one for saving.

5
Show its limits
Talk through your own shopping choices, showing how you make decisions about what is and isn't good value. Such chats will make it clear that you can't afford everything you want.

7
Explain card spending
In an increasingly cashless world, explain that when you use a card, it's the same as having money taken out of your bank account.

8
Let them make mistakes
Even if you disagree with his spending decisions, allow your child to make mistakes. It's better to learn with small amounts at a young age, than bigger amounts later on.

10
Don't tie it to chores
Don't make your child earn pocket money. It sends him a confusing message that he should be paid for something he should do anyway.

11
Be consistent
Give children pocket money at the same time each week in the same way as a salary, so they can start to manage their money.

12
Don't give it upfront
Try not to pay out in advance. If they ask, charge a small amount of interest so they realize it costs money to borrow money.

"Stop fighting!"

Most parents will argue in front of their children at some point. It can be difficult to think clearly when emotions are running high, but how you handle these conflicts is crucial for your child's wellbeing and their understanding of how relationships work.

SCENARIO | During an argument with your partner, your child shouts at you both to stop fighting.

SHE SAYS

"Stop fighting!"

YOU MIGHT THINK

"I'm so angry. I don't care if my child sees."

Your child may not understand the reasons, but she still registers the conflict. Studies show that even young babies show a rise in blood pressure and stress hormones when they hear their parents shouting in anger. She depends on you for everything so, to her, this feels like an earthquake.

Instinctively you know that it's upsetting for your child to see you arguing, but you can't stop yourself as your brain is now in "primal mode" – when the reactive, fight-or-flight part of your brain takes over and overcomes your rational thinking.

VIEW YOU AND YOUR PARTNER AS BEING ON THE SAME TEAM, AND AN ARGUMENT AS A PROBLEM TO BE SOLVED, NOT A CONTEST TO WIN.

WHAT SHE'S THINKING

"What will happen to me if they break up?"

Your child believes that adults in relationships should be loving all the time, so if she hears you say cruel things to each other, she may think you're splitting up. Children tend to believe the world revolves around them, so she is likely to assume that the row is about her.

SEE RELATED TOPICS

But Mummy said I could: pp.186–187
I wish I had a different family: pp.194–195

HOW TO RESPOND

In the moment...

Calm yourself There are always two problems in an argument: your emotions running out of control and the actual problem. Protect your child from witnessing the former by recognizing when your reactive "lower brain" has taken over. Show your child you are calming down and say that you and your partner will talk about it later.

Reassure her Above all, children want to feel safe, so tell your child an argument doesn't mean you don't love each other. Acknowledge the disagreement, making it clear that it wasn't her fault, even if you were arguing about something connected to her. Say: "Daddy and I were angry with each other. Now we're working it out."

Use the conflict to teach your child about emotions If they see you make up and move on, children can learn that even happy couples disagree, anger is a normal emotion, there's nothing wrong with expressing it, and communicating well can resolve disputes.

In the long term...

Don't drive it underground You may think it's better not to show open conflict, but using passive aggressive tactics, such as the silent treatment, is more confusing to children who still pick up on the tension.

Look for ways to sort out your differences If a child keeps witnessing unresolved rows, it can trigger anxiety, sleep disturbances, concentration problems, and difficulties with peers. After a row, write down everything that caused it, without blame or accusation, so you can talk it through with your partner calmly.

"But I'm not tired."

Even though getting enough sleep is essential for their growth, health, and learning, children spend a lot of effort fighting going to bed. This battle can be even more difficult if your child is in the habit of playing screen-based games before bedtime.

SCENARIO | **It's time for bed, but your child is refusing to stop playing his computer game.**

SLEEP IS JUST AS IMPORTANT AS HEALTHY EATING AND EXERCISE FOR DEVELOPMENT.

HE SAYS

"But I'm not tired."

At this age, children may no longer feel "little" so feel entitled to stay up later. As peer pressure starts to increase, children this age may also brag to each other about how late they are allowed to stay up and your child may want you to believe you send him to bed unfairly early compared with his peers.

SEE RELATED TOPICS
It's not fair: pp.180–181
You never let me do anything: pp.238–239

YOU MIGHT THINK

"I could really do without this after a long day. Plus he'll wake up grumpy tomorrow."

WHAT HE'S THINKING

"I'm a big boy now. Games are more exciting than going to sleep."

You may be dreading the row that's coming because the immediate gratification of a computer game makes it hard for your child to pull himself away. You're likely to be right that he won't sleep as well and will wake up more bad-tempered.

The blue light emitted by electronics interrupts sleep-inducing hormones, so your child may genuinely not feel sleepy. Fast-moving graphics also rev up his brain, so he finds it much harder to transition to sleep.

HOW TO RESPOND

In the moment...

Give him a countdown Stay calm and give your child a five-minute warning so he can finish his game and prepare for the transition. Video games can over-stimulate his brain, so he will be more reactive if you lose your temper.

Offer time with you instead Though he may protest to start with, most of all, your child wants one-on-one time with you. Present screen-free time as a reward, not a punishment.

In the long term...

Introduce a digital sunset Make sure your child does not use electronic gadgets for at least an hour before bedtime, so his sleep hormones kick in. Reintroduce the ritual of bath and bedtime stories, if this has slipped.

Reset his bedtime As they get older and have more to do after school, childrens' bedtime routines can fall apart and their mood, concentration, and schoolwork can suffer. Reset the time your child goes to bed by counting back 10½ hours from when he gets up. Then stick to it.

Help him see the benefits of sleep Point out how much better your child feels when he has had a good night's sleep so he sees the connection for himself. The more you talk to your child about your reasons at neutral times, the more he will see it's for his own benefit.

"I'm bored."

Children are usually bursting with enthusiasm, so when your child says she's bored, you can feel worried that you are not stimulating her enough. But children need to be left to their own devices, so that they learn to direct themselves.

SCENARIO | **Your child says there is nothing to do and she's not interested in any of her toys or games.**

SHE SAYS

"I'm bored."

YOU MIGHT THINK

"She's got so much stuff. Do I have to entertain her every second?"

Boredom can be a good thing – it's a sign your child has the free time to do whatever she likes. The catch-all phrase of "I'm bored" could be used by children to mean other things: trying to bring up a topic that's bothering them, feeling flat but not knowing why, or wanting attention.

Many parents fall into the trap of believing they must be constantly "building" their child's brain with all sorts of activities. But research shows that having nothing to do stimulates a child's thinking and boost creativity. Don't feel guilty about her complaints of boredom.

" "

LEARNING HOW TO BEAT BOREDOM IS A CRUCIAL LIFE SKILL. IT TAKES EFFORT AND PRACTICE TO WORK OUT WHAT TO DO WITH THEMSELVES.

WHAT SHE'S THINKING

"There's no school, no screens, and only myself to play with. What am I supposed to do now?"

Sometimes children complain of boredom if they're looking for something to fully engage their brain or if they're unsure of what to do next. Over time, your child will get better at working out what to do without adult guidance and, in doing so, will get to know herself better.

HOW TO RESPOND

In the moment...

Acknowledge her feelings Listen and tell her you know what it feels like. Tell her that while boredom may feel unfamiliar and uncomfortable, that feeling will soon pass when she lets her brain guide her towards a new activity.

Don't come up with every solution If your child has the usual options – toys, books, craft materials, and going outside to play – it's not your job to "fix" her boredom. Let her come up with her own ideas.

Challenge your child Suggest she writes a list of all her toys, so she remembers what she has, digs out some of her old ones, or creates something and shows you. This will guide her towards exploring activities on her own but also reassure her she has an interested audience. Praise her efforts.

In the long term...

Let go of the guilt Instead of feeling like "having nothing to do" is a failing on your part, see it as a chance for your child to daydream, decompress, and let their imagination run free.

Set aside more free play Research shows that extracurricular activities mean children have far less unstructured time than ever before. This can leave children feeling at a loss when they do have some. Give your child more free time, so she develops hobbies and pastimes to entertain herself.

SEE RELATED TOPICS
Homework is boring: pp.202–203
After-school activities: pp.244–245

"I'm not as good as them."

For the parent of a child who has only just started "proper" lessons at school, it can be worrying to hear him say he already can't keep up. How you react can keep your child's self-belief strong and sustain his motivation to continue learning.

SCENARIO | **Your child says he is on the yellow table where all the children who find maths hard sit.**

HE SAYS

"I'm not as good as them."

YOU MIGHT THINK

"His confidence is so low. Should I get him a tutor?"

Now your child is at school, surrounded by a class of other children, he is starting to understand that others have different skills and is comparing himself with them. His self-appraisal, though painful to hear, is a natural part of his development and it's now more important than ever to support his self-belief.

It's easy to feel panicked when you hear your child say he feels his skills are lesser. You may worry that if he is already struggling, he will always struggle and if you don't "fix" this, he will lose confidence and stop trying.

SEE RELATED TOPICS
I don't want to go to school: pp.196–197
I'm not pretty enough: pp.242–243

EXPLAIN THAT IT'S BEST TO COMPETE WITH HIMSELF NOT WITH OTHERS BECAUSE HE WILL IMPROVE AND ALWAYS WIN.

WHAT HE'S THINKING

"I'm not good at maths now, so I never will be."

Children this age are "always" or "never" thinkers. So, your child may believe that because he does not excel at maths at this moment, he never will. He may also internalize this message (as negative self-talk), so it keeps popping into his head, which in turn makes it harder for him to think clearly when he does have maths to do.

HOW TO RESPOND

In the moment...

Listen and acknowledge While it may be tempting to say "Don't be silly; you're very clever," instead it's better to acknowledge rather than dismiss his feelings. Explain, too, that different children learn at different speeds but they all master the same skills eventually.

Be warm and understanding Don't be tempted to be a "tiger" parent here. Strengthening his belief in himself as an effective learner will work better to support him than introducing measures to improve his academic performance, which may only increase his anxiety.

Avoid reinforcing the message You may want to comfort your child by sharing the fact that you weren't good at maths at school. But this sends the message that he's destined to find maths difficult. Instead give examples of how you improved by applying yourself.

In the long term...

Praise the effort When you see him do his maths homework, compliment him for the effort he puts in.

Reinforce other talents Remind your child there are lots of ways of being "clever" that don't relate to school.

"I've got a boyfriend."

As they become more aware of the differences between boys and girls, children prefer to play with friends of the same gender. However, if they have a friend of the opposite sex, some may copy adults by calling each other "boyfriend" or "girlfriend".

SCENARIO | **Your child comes home with a card from a boy in her class, saying: "To my girlfriend".**

SHE SAYS

"I've got a boyfriend."

YOU MIGHT THINK

"She's too young for a boyfriend. Where is she getting this idea from?"

A boyfriend in this sense is most likely to be a boy who is a friend; she is not referring to someone she is sexually attracted to. But because they've labelled each other as "girlfriend" and "boyfriend" they may give each other a hug or a peck on the cheek.

You may be shocked that she seems to have a romantic relationship. But at this age, children are role-playing what they see adults doing in the world. Since she's reached a stage of development where she can role-play scenarios that she hasn't yet experienced she may even say they "got married".

VALUE ALL YOUR CHILD'S RELATIONSHIPS EQUALLY. EXPLAIN A FRIEND IS A FRIEND NO MATTER WHAT SEX THEY ARE.

WHAT SHE'S THINKING

He's a boy and he's my friend, so isn't he my boyfriend?"

Your child is exploring how the "rules" of society work and may well have overheard grown-ups talking about boyfriends and girlfriends. Or she may be moving towards a more polarized view of gender and believes she needs a boyfriend to be truly female. Most children won't think anything of playing with the opposite gender until they are made more self-conscious about it by adults.

SEE RELATED TOPICS

They're being mean to me: pp.192–193
She's my best friend: pp.198–199

HOW TO RESPOND

In the moment...

Ask what she means Find out what your child means by "boyfriend". It may be wishful thinking on her part or the other child may not realize how he's being described.

Explain the difference Tell her that a friend who's a boy is not the same as a "boyfriend". Explain that only older people have boyfriend or girlfriend relationships.

Don't elaborate Resist telling your child how adorable it is to have a boyfriend. Also avoid describing this friendship in adult terms or playing up its importance by teasing her or asking for progress reports.

In the long term...

Arrange a play date If your child and her boyfriend genuinely seem to be friends, organize a play date. You'll soon see how they play together.

Encourage lots of friendships At this age, children are becoming more conscious of their status within a peer group. Your child may feel the need to impress, look "special", or feel socially sophisticated by saying she has a boyfriend. If you think she's trying to bolster her status, help her build her self-worth in other ways and help her develop a wide circle of friends.

"I'm not playing any more!"

Parents are often pleased to see their child showing their first signs of competitive spirit. But while you may want your child to be able to hold his own and strive for his goals, being too competitive can come at a cost to his social relationships.

SCENARIO | Your child says he no longer wants to play a game of cards with a friend because he is losing.

HE SAYS

"I'm not playing any more!"

Up until the age of about 4, children are happy to play cooperatively and help each other. However, as a child's social group expands, he will start to compare his abilities with others, resulting in the start of more openly competitive behaviour.

YOUR CHILD MAY NOT REALIZE IT'S SOMETIMES BETTER TO LOSE A GAME THAN A FRIEND.

YOU MIGHT THINK

"He needs to learn to compete. But if he can't stand losing, no one will want to play with him."

You may believe that your child needs a winner-takes-all attitude to get ahead, but he still needs to learn not to bend the rules and how to tolerate his frustration and aggressive instincts.

SEE RELATED TOPICS
No one likes me: pp.190–191
I'm the best: pp.204–205

WHAT HE'S THINKING

"It's not fun when I lose. I'd do anything to win."

Your child is now trying to find his place in the social hierarchy. If he has a dominant personality, he may want to be top dog and winning is one way to pull rank and impress others. He may not yet have learned that his drive to do well has to be balanced by a willingness to play cooperatively.

HOW TO RESPOND

In the moment...

Talk about how to cope with losing Tell your child that no one can win all the time and next time the result might be different. If he has a meltdown over losing, say: "I understand you're upset, but it's just a game and you need to control your frustration."

Emphasize teamwork Talk about how cooperation and mutual respect for fellow players is just as important as the drive to win. Ask him: "How can you change how you play that will keep it fun for everyone?"

Discuss good sportsmanship Explain to your child that he should keep playing fairly even if he's losing, or others won't want to play. Give him examples of professional sportspeople losing with dignity and good grace.

In the long term...

Check your messages Are you passing on ideas that it's a cut-throat world and your child must win at any cost? Be aware of what messages you might be sending.

Practise games with older children Encourage him to play board games with older children who can model good behaviour and show him that he can still enjoy playing without needing to win every time.

The digital world

Your child is growing up as a digital native. As the use of technology becomes ever-more normal, children are on devices and going online earlier. It's crucial that parents "teach" them to be tech savvy at all ages.

While many children may feel confident about using the internet, their understanding of the world is not developed enough to fully understand all the risks. That's why your input and support is vital.

Seeing the potential

Not all screen-time is created equal; you can watch passively, engage actively, communicate via video or message, or be creative. So, view technology as an extra resource – enjoy footage of the natural world, play an app together, have a regular slot to stay in touch with grandparents, and get homework help.

Ensure time online does not take away time from other activities, such as reading books, drawing, and playing outside. And you'll need to manage your child's digital use, as she's wired for novelty and can't control that.

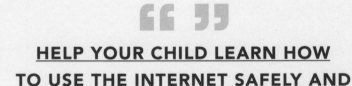

HELP YOUR CHILD LEARN HOW TO USE THE INTERNET SAFELY AND APPROPRIATELY FOR HER AGE.

1
Limit screen-time
Research shows it's a good idea to have no more than 1 hour of screen-time of high-quality apps or games a day for 2–5-year-olds.

4
Search in safety
Set up a favourites list of agreed websites and kid-safe search engines, so her search results are age appropriate.

6
Use tech for good
Learn, create, and connect with your child, rather than passively entertaining her.

9
Say "no" to a phone
Phones are powerful mini-computers. While kids may already be asking for a phone, it's too early to give them this sort of capacity. Wait until they hit double digits.

GOOD PRACTICE

12 key principles

2
Set a good example
Set aside time with your children when you are not using your phone and be a good role model with your own digital use.

3
Have screen-free times
Keep mealtimes, coming-home times, and days out tech-free so devices don't interrupt family time. Children don't have a problem with this if the whole family complies.

5
Buy an alarm clock
Your child could be tempted to use a tablet when she should be sleeping if she takes it to her bedroom. And a "digital sunset" (a rule of no screens for an hour before bed) can help to avoid light disrupting sleep.

7
Make tech visible
Keep devices in common areas, such as the kitchen, so you can see how she's using the internet and share her discoveries.

8
Keep talking
Let her know you're informed about the online world. Ask about what she's seen online today or what games she's playing to engage her in digital experiences.

10
Know to put it down
If your child sees anything upsetting or distressing, tell her to close the laptop or turn the tablet face down, and go tell an adult.

11
Respect age restrictions
The minimum age for many social media sites is 13. Giving access before then means she may not be ready for the things she's exposed to there.

12
No electronic nanny
Never put your child to bed with a device. They need a story with you both for language and social development and for them to feel valued.

TAILORED ADVICE
Age by age
2–3
YEAR-OLDS
You decide
Young children are fascinated by digital devices, but your child will not be "behind" if you decide to wait to introduce these.

Keep it active and brief
If you want your child to explore using digital devices, do it together. Play with photos or video and find age-appropriate apps that allow her to take an active role. Keep sessions under half an hour.

4–5
YEAR-OLDS
Screen-free rewards
Tell your child how much you love to play games where you play directly with one another – Snap or Snakes and Ladders – rather than have a screen in the way.

Help with homework
Kids use computers most days at school, so be prepared for her to use a device to continue her work at home.

6–7
YEAR-OLDS
Privacy is paramount
Explain that she must never give out personal information or share private photos.

Give the whole picture
Children don't realize their web use is tracked by online sites and used to show them ads, so explain how that works.

"Where do babies come from?"

At this age, children are starting to hear from their friends about how grown-ups make babies. Be ready to explain sex in a sensitive, age-appropriate way, so your child doesn't get confused or worried.

SCENARIO | **Your child has heard from his friends about how mummies and daddies make babies. He wants to know if it's true.**

HE SAYS

"Where do babies come from?"

Children are now curious about their place in the world and where they came from. If they don't get the facts, they may use "magical thinking", which means they make up a story to explain what they don't yet understand. For example, they may imagine that when someone wants a baby all they have to do is go to the hospital and ask for one.

SEE RELATED TOPICS

What's a stranger?: pp.232–233
My diary – keep out!: pp.234–235

YOU MIGHT THINK

"He's too young to know about anything so grown-up. I don't want to say the wrong thing."

You may feel nervous because you want to get the wording right first time and you don't want to scare your child. You may also be uncomfortable about revealing an intimate side of yourself to your child and feel embarrassed they will work out this was how you conceived them.

WHAT HE'S THINKING

"I've heard kids talk about the daddy putting his willy into the mummy to make a baby, but that can't be true."

Your child is now more aware of the differences between boys and girls. What he has heard may sound bizarre or even disgusting to him. He may be asking for reassurance that the truth is not as strange as it sounds. But, at this stage, he can only handle an introduction to the simple mechanics of reproduction.

HOW TO RESPOND

In the moment...

Ask your child how much he knows Ask him where he thinks babies come from. Once you understand his level of knowledge you will be able to respond with the right words and clear up any misunderstandings.

Give the basics Use straightforward language you are comfortable with. For instance, say: "A special type of seed, called sperm, comes out of a daddy's penis and swims up a mummy's vagina to find her egg. When they meet, a baby can start to grow."

Stop at the right time If your child reacts with a "yuck", laugh along and says it's what grown-ups sometimes do to feel close and show love. Stop the conversation if there are no more questions. It means they have enough information and `need time to process it.

In the long term...

Keep talking As your child gets older, let the topic come up naturally again so you can add more context, such as how sex is something nice for adults who love each other. Say you understand if it sounds confusing, but assure your child it will make sense as he gets older.

Use other resources If you find it hard to find the words, use books specifically written by experts to educate children about sex to guide conversations and discussions with your child.

"Do I have to do music practice?"

Music lessons are often seen as some of the best gifts you can give a child. Research suggests playing a musical instrument benefits coordination as well as social and emotional development. The challenge is working out how to fit it all into family life.

SCENARIO | Your child says she hates practising the piano and complains about having to go to music lessons at all.

SHE SAYS

"Do I have to do music practice?"

After a long day at school, music practice Pcan seem like a lot of effort for a child, who wants downtime after school and homework. Parents, on the other hand, tend to see the bigger picture and view the challenge and discipline of learning an instrument as good training. But differences in approach can lead to conflict with your child.

SEE RELATED TOPICS
It's not fair: pp.180–181
Homework is boring: pp.202–203

YOU MIGHT THINK

"It's a competitive world out there. She's got to start young to be any good or get ahead."

You may believe that if your child starts young and practises enough, she could be a music prodigy – or win a music scholarship when she's older. While it's great to offer such opportunities, you need to be realistic. You will end up in a power struggle if the motivation comes only from you.

WHAT SHE'S THINKING

"I never have time to just sit at home and do what I want to do."

Children have lots of energy but they also need downtime and free play. Your child may be complaining because she feels the desire to play the piano comes more from you, than from her. If music is not one of her "sparks", she may enjoy an activity more in line with her temperament.

HOW TO RESPOND

In the moment...

①

Be encouraging Be an appreciative audience at all times, however hard your child's early attempts are on the ears. If your child feels criticized, she will become self-conscious about practising.

②

Praise her persistence Listen together to recordings of the piece your child is working on, however simple it is, so she is motivated and knows how it is supposed to sound. Talk about how every day she practises, she gets a tiny bit closer to creating music as good as that.

In the long term...

Keep practice times short Put her instrument in a communal area of the house, so she does not feel lonely practising in her bedroom. Short daily sessions of 10 minutes work better than the occasional half hour.

Join in Treat music practice as a bonding time to have fun with your child. Get involved in musical games, such as creating a lucky dip game for her pieces, or put small stickers on her music every time she plays it.

Be flexible Your child may start on the piano and then want to switch to guitar later on because she can play along to more songs she likes with her friends. She has still built up her coordination and musical understanding.

"What's a stranger?"

When your child was a baby and then a toddler, he was always with you or a trusted adult. Now he's becoming more independent, you may worry about his safety in the wider world. Equipping him with the skills he needs will help keep him safe.

SCENARIO | **During a family trip to the beach, your child asks if he can get an ice cream. You tell him not to go off with a stranger.**

HE SAYS

"What's a stranger?"

YOU MIGHT THINK

"I don't want him to worry, but what if something happened?"

Because your child has always been surrounded by people he feels are there to look after him, he is likely to believe that all adults are safe. It may be both shocking and confusing to hear you say that some grown-ups might not always have his best interests at heart.

As a parent, your first instinct is to protect your child, but even thinking about abduction can trigger intense anxiety in you. You may also be nervous of him asking about what happens when a stranger abducts a child, and how to explain this without destroying his innocence.

AS YOUR CHILD BECOMES MORE INDEPENDENT, FIND A MIDDLE GROUND BETWEEN KEEPING HIM SAFE AND ALLOWING HIM TO EXPLORE THE WORLD.

HOW TO RESPOND

In the moment...

Explain simply Rather than talk about evil "baddies" and what they are capable of, explain that while most people they do not know are good, there are some who aren't and who don't want to keep children safe.

②

Avoid saying "don't talk to strangers" Children need to know it's OK to talk to people in shops or on public transport, or to ask for help. Suggest instead they look out for behaviour that makes them feel uncomfortable, such as a much older child, teen, or grown-up asking them for help, instead of asking an adult. Teach them to watch for "uh-oh" feelings and to listen to those before worrying about being polite, even with other children.

In the long term...

Coach him When you're out with your child, play "what if" quizzes asking him what he would do in different situations, for example: "What if you got lost in a big shop?"

Tell him to ask you Children this age may be confused about what a stranger looks like and may not understand that some will seem friendly and charming. Ask your child to always "check first" with you or the person looking after them if someone they don't know asks them to do something.

Keep perspective Don't allow your anxieties to get in the way of letting your child explore the wider world. Being abducted by a stranger is rare. Give equal priority to teaching him other safety skills, such as how to swim, cross the road, and stay safe online.

WHAT HE'S THINKING

"Why would a stranger want to hurt me? How do I know who they are?"

Your child still has an abstract awareness of evil, such as imaginary monsters that embody his general fears of the unknown, and giving "evil" a human form can be disturbing. Children can't rationalize in the same way as adults, so it's important to keep his anxiety in perspective.

► SEE RELATED TOPICS ◄
Where do babies come from?: pp.228–229
I want a phone: pp.240–241

"My diary – keep out!"

As your child starts to understand her own personal thoughts and feelings better, she may start to write a diary in which she can express things she wants to keep private. While it may be tempting to read her diary, it's best to respect her privacy.

SCENARIO | **You're tidying your child's bedroom and notice a notebook by her bed titled "My diary – keep out!"**

SHE SAYS

"My diary – keep out!"

YOU MIGHT THINK

"Why can't she tell me everything? Doesn't she trust me?"

At this age, your child is experiencing a wider range of contradictory feelings. By putting them on paper, she is externalizing, organizing, and processing them, which makes her feel better. Children this age have magical thinking: she believes that writing "keep out" will be enough to stop you looking.

Your child is now learning she can choose what she shares. You may worry that she has something to hide, or that she no longer trusts you, but her diary is part of the necessary process of separation as she continues her journey to adulthood.

YOUR CHILD IS STARTING TO LEARN THERE ARE BOUNDARIES BETWEEN WHAT SHE THINKS AND WHAT SHE TELLS YOU AND OTHER PEOPLE.

WHAT SHE'S THINKING

"I don't want to tell Mummy and Daddy everything. I like having thoughts others don't know about."

A diary is your child's safe place to express all her feelings, including uncomfortable ones such as hatred or jealousy, which are often disapproved of by adults. At this age, your child's writing skills and memory have also improved so she'll find it exciting that she's now able to create a private space where she can say what she likes freely, without adult censure.

SEE RELATED TOPICS
I hate you: pp.184–185
You're embarrassing me: pp.206–207

HOW TO RESPOND

In the moment...

Don't read it If your child finds out you have read her diary, you risk her losing her trust. In any case, it's likely to be a basic retelling of the events of her day.

Welcome it Don't see your child's diary as a way to exclude you. Be pleased that she is in touch with her feelings enough to write them down. Research has found that keeping a diary reduces stress and improves health.

In the long term...

Talk about good and bad secrets Explain that a bad secret would make her feel sad, worried, or frightened, whereas a good secret, such as a surprise party or present, would make her feel excited. Emphasize that she needs to chat to a grown-up if she has a bad secret.

Stay connected If you feel out of touch with your child's life, fill in the gaps by connecting with her, rather than reading her diary. Choose neutral settings to chat, such as in the car or while walking to and from school. Let her know you are always there when she wants to talk.

Value all emotions Don't disapprove of emotions such as hatred or jealousy just because they make you uncomfortable. If you do, your child may feel that she can't express herself freely with you. Explain that it's how she handles these feelings that is important.

"Why do you have to go to work?"

Your child is still biologically wired to want to stay close to you, so when your job takes you away or intrudes into the time you have together, he may feel resentful. You may not be able to choose how much you work, but you can limit its impact on your home life.

SCENARIO | You have to catch the early train to get to work and won't be able to take your child to school.

HE SAYS

"Why do you have to go to work?"

YOU MIGHT THINK

"Have I got my priorities wrong?"

This question is a sign that your child is starting to see your work as a threat to your time together. He may also not like your work if he notices that it makes you stressed and distracted or it means you sometimes can't be at important events, such as school assemblies.

Hearing this may trigger a mixture of emotions. You may worry that you're damaging your child by not being there enough, or that you are missing out on his childhood. That said, you may also feel you need to work for your self-esteem or to safeguard your future.

LOOK FOR WAYS TO RING-FENCE FAMILY TIME SO YOUR CHILD KNOWS HE IS YOUR PRIORITY.

WHAT HE'S THINKING

"Maybe Mummy loves work more than me?"

Your child believes that adults have choice over everything, so he will see your job as something you choose to do without him. At this age, children are still getting to grips with how much you have to work to earn the money you need. As a result, your child may process your work as a rejection.

HOW TO RESPOND

In the moment...

Be understanding While your child's question may trigger guilt, remember that he is not saying this to make you feel bad. Children tend to believe the world revolves around them, so it is natural for him to want assurance that you love him more than anything else.

Talk through your feelings Explain that while work is never more important, you also need to do useful things and meet new people just as he does at school. Tell him that work also allows you to earn money, which means you can provide for him. Tell him you are always thinking of him when you are not together.

Help your child understand what you do Talk about different jobs and relate them to your child's experience. For example, talk about how the teachers and catering staff at his school help him during his day.

In the long term...

Check your priorities Use this opportunity to think more about how work impacts your home life. If you feel it is affecting how you are with your child, ring-fence your time together, for example, by only dealing with work emails after your child's bedtime.

Be a mindful parent When you come home, visualize yourself letting go of the working day and embracing your role as parent. Build in more one-on-one time and make the most of weekends, as well as holidays, to show your child how much you love being with him.

SEE RELATED TOPICS
I have to tell you something: pp.178–179
I don't want to go to school: pp.196–197

"You never let me do anything."

At this age, your child may want to start trying new things for herself to feel more grown-up and part of her peer group. This new-found independence may bring up many different – possibly conflicting – feelings for you as a parent.

SCENARIO | **After school, your child says her new friend has asked her to come to her dad's house for a sleepover, but you say "No".**

SHE SAYS

"You never let me do anything."

YOU MIGHT THINK

"She's still so little. I'm trying to keep her safe."

Your child is becoming aware of her place in the world. She wants to spend more time with her peers and have more freedom. A sleepover is an exciting new thing that she is desperate to do with her new friend and to feel more grown-up.

As a parent, you are used to controlling your child's environment completely, with safety in mind. So, to let another adult, and one you don't know, be in charge feels unfamiliar and worrying. Saying "No" may have relieved your anxiety.

IF WE TRY TO HOLD BACK CHILDREN'S INDEPENDENCE THEY NEVER LEARN TO NEGOTIATE RISKS.

WHAT SHE'S THINKING

"All my friends get to go on sleepovers. I'm not a baby."

Your child may believe other parents are more lenient, or say so to make you doubt yourself. Even if she's nervous about spending a night away, she doesn't want to seem babyish to her peers. That said, while she may appear furious, children feel safe when parents set fair and thoughtful parameters.

HOW TO RESPOND

In the moment...

Check why you are saying "No" As a parent, you may have a blind spot about letting your child have more independence. Keep your decisions grounded in what you know, rather than what you fear. If you find yourself saying "No" almost as a reflex response to your child's requests, you may want to reconsider if it's time to give her more freedom.

State the boundaries Make it clear that while you are pleased your child feels confident enough to sleep away from home and you want her to have fun, all arrangements need to be agreed between parents first.

Explain your decision Place yourself as an authoritative parent who will give all of your child's requests consideration. You can still say "No", but her emotional and social development will benefit if you explain why.

In the long term...

Get to know other parents The African proverb: "It takes a village to raise a child" is a good prompt. You will feel more comfortable letting your child branch out if you make a conscious effort to get to know the families of other children in her class.

Beware of being a helicopter parent Resist the temptation to hover too much over your child's life beyond the point where it is necessary. If you are too anxious, your child assumes she is incapable and that there must be a lot to worry about.

SEE RELATED TOPICS
It's not fair: pp.180–181
I wish I had a different family: pp.194–195

"I want a phone."

Even though most parents wait until their child reaches double figures to give him or her a phone, that may not stop yours asking for one if he thinks it will impress his peers or keep him constantly entertained.

SCENARIO | **Your child says he really needs a phone for his birthday.**

HE SAYS

"I want a phone."

YOU MIGHT THINK

"Maybe I should get him a phone. It could help keep him safe."

To a child, a phone seems to be the ultimate toy. He wants it to play games, take photos, and send messages, just as you do. He is not yet mature enough to realize that phones can be absorbing and interfere with the real-world interaction, play, and physical activity he needs for healthy development.

You may be tempted to give your child a phone so that you can contact him easily at all times, especially if you and your co-parent live separately. You may also feel like a good parent because you can buy him high-value gadgets or think it may help him impress his peers.

LET YOUR CHILD ENJOY THE FUN AND INNOCENCE OF CHILDHOOD BEFORE YOU ALLOW A PHONE TO DISTRACT HIM FROM REAL-WORLD EXPERIENCES.

WHAT HE'S THINKING

> "My friends would think I was so cool if I had my own phone. I'd feel so grown up."

Your child lives in a world in which everyone else appears to be on their phone, so it's natural for him to want one too. His reputation among his peers is also increasingly important to him and the pressure to look "cool" has kicked in, so he thinks having a phone will buy him status.

SEE RELATED TOPICS

No one likes me: pp.190–191
But all my friends have one: pp.208–209

HOW TO RESPOND

In the moment...

Say no Explain that he has to wait until he's older and the reasons why. Tell him that phones are not toys. They are powerful mini-computers that open up a vast adult world into which he is too young to venture.

Explain the cost Many children assume phones are free. They also tend to think a phone is a right they are entitled to, rather than something they have to prove they are ready for. Tell your child phones are expensive and that they are a privilege he may get when he is older.

Ask why he wants one Find out what difference your child thinks having a phone will make. Is he trying to earn social credibility? If so, he may be struggling to fit in. Help him find different ways of building friendships by encouraging play dates and helping him practise social skills, such as sharing and taking turns.

In the long term...

Make the real world more interesting Engage with your child and point out the wonders of real life. Prioritize fun family time throughout his childhood so screens don't seem more exciting.

Model balanced phone use If you are glued to your phone and behave as if it's the centre of your universe, your child might get a disproportionate idea of its importance and believe he can't live without one either.

"I'm not pretty enough."

Children are exposed to more images of physical perfection now than in the past. Without adult guidance, children can feel they are failing if they are allowed to believe they do not live up to society's ideals. But there are lots of ways to counteract such messages.

SCENARIO | **Your child is crying because she says she's not as pretty as the people she sees on TV.**

SHE SAYS

"I'm not pretty enough."

As children grow up, adults tend to comment on girls' appearance more than boys', who tend to be complimented on assertiveness and strength. It can mean girls grow up thinking that appearance is the most important thing. If your child has heard you criticize your own looks, she may have internalized this negative voice and applied it to herself.

❝ ❞

PARENTS HAVE A KEY ROLE IN ENSURING CHILDREN VALUE THEMSELVES FOR THEIR QUALITIES, NOT THEIR LOOKS.

SEE RELATED TOPICS
I can't do it: pp.182–183
I'm not as good as them: pp.220–221

YOU MIGHT THINK

"She's beautiful. How can she think such a thing about herself at such a young age?"

WHAT SHE'S THINKING

"Why don't I look like the models and pop stars I see on TV and online?"

Parents often feel caught in the headlights when they hear their child express such feelings. You may be panicked by media stories about body image and how even children are affected. And you may worry about saying the wrong thing, she could spiral into super-self-consciousness.

Children used to have a more realistic view of how people looked from just seeing the people around them. In a world where celebrity culture is all pervading, she lacks the perspective to know how manipulated these images are.

HOW TO RESPOND

In the moment...

Ask her why Give her a cuddle and find out why she thinks she's not pretty enough and who's she comparing herself to. Ask her to name three things she likes about her body, and you do the same about yours.

Value other qualities Describe her uniqueness and talk about the amazing things her body can do, not what it looks like. Be careful to never pass comment on yours or anyone else's body shape or size in front of your child.

In the long term...

Talk about healthy bodies Explain that her child's body is not supposed to look like a grown-up's body – their shapes are different and features mature with time.

Be kinder to yourself Refrain from criticizing your appearance, talking about dieting, or weighing yourself in front of your child. Let your child hear you compliment yourself – and others – on other qualities, such as honesty, kindness, or a sense of humour.

Help her filter the messages Children do not yet have the life experience to understand that celebrity images are not realistic or to understand how they make them feel. Look through a magazine together to show your child how pictures of models may have been altered.

After-school activities

It's natural for parents to want their children to try various activities, so they grow into well-rounded adults. After-school lessons and clubs can help kids build on their talents as well as meet new friends with similar interests.

It's incredibly important for children to have unscheduled playtime to learn, problem solve, process their emotions, and discover for themselves how the world works. So, always balance activities around other playdates and free time.

Some extras, such as Beavers and Cubs, or Brownies, are helpful for building important life skills, such as teamwork, and get children out among nature. Every child should learn how to swim, so classes taught by properly trained staff are important.

Children will tend to stick at activities – and stay with them for longer – if they are based on their "spark", or what your child is naturally drawn to play with. Keep an eye out for her talents and use extracurricular activities to develop these.

" "

WHEN CHILDREN FIND AN ACTIVITY THAT DEVELOPS INTO A SKILL, THEY FEEL MORE COMPETENT, WHICH BOOSTS SELF-WORTH.

1
Have a trial first
Ask for a taster session of a new after-school activity to find out if your child shows an interest and enjoys it before signing them up.

4
Ignore FOMO
When parents see others signing their kids up to an activity, they can experience "fear of missing out" and feel their child will miss out, too. Be sure to base your decisions on your child's interests.

7
Monitor your stress levels
If you find yourself rushing from one activity to another and are starting to feel overwhelmed, chances are your child is overwhelmed, too.

9
TIY – teach it yourself
For activities that can easily be done at home – cooking or art and craft – your child would probably rather learn by doing them with you.

GOOD PRACTICE

10 key principles

2
Check them out
Many businesses offer a range of child-centred activities. Speak to the instructors to check they are qualified and that enjoyment is put before profit.

3
Match the activity to your child
Children should get at least an hour of moderate exercise a day. Ask your child which physical activity she would like to do. While some kids prefer team sports, such as football, others will prefer individual pursuits, such as dance or cycling.

5
Watch for signs of too much on
Children may not tell parents they want to give up an activity for fear of disappointing them. Think about cutting back if your child says she'd like more time at home, seems constantly tired, or suffers from tummy or headaches.

6
Be flexible
As your child grows, let her activities grow with her. Rather than worry about lack of staying power, view moving onto a new activity as an opportunity for her to try something new and build on skills she has already learned.

8
Check your motives
Have you signed your child up to an activity because you think your child really likes it – or because you think it gives her an advantage? If so, she may pick up on the pressure and feel anxious.

10
Give them daily downtime
A range of studies has found that unstructured play helps children to regulate emotions, make plans, and solve problems. Make sure your child has time every day for free play that does not involve screens.

TAILORED ADVICE
Age by age

2–3
YEAR-OLDS
One-on-one time
At this age most children learn better from one-on-one fun interaction with a parent or carer, than larger group activities, which can be overwhelming. A trip to the park, playing games, and singing nursery rhymes with you is just as exciting and rewarding as a structured music class

4–5
YEAR-OLDS
Settling in
Since children are only just getting used to the school routine, avoid starting any new classes in the first term.

Play comes first
Your child is still getting to know classmates and needs practice with sharing and turn-taking, so prioritize playdates now.

6–7
YEAR-OLDS
More school-based fun
Steer children towards extracurricular activities they can do in school break and lunchtimes, so they don't eat into downtime after school.

Getting enough sleep?
At this age children should be getting 9–11 hours. Cut back on activities if your child is often finishing homework late or going to bed past her bedtime.

Bibliography

024–025 HOW CHILDREN LEARN
B. Hart and T. R. Risley, *Meaningful Differences in the Everyday Experience of Young American Children*, Baltimore, Brookes Publishing, 1995.

026–027 YOUR CHILD'S BRAIN
M. M. Tanaka-Arakawa et al., "Developmental Changes in the Corpus Callosum from Infancy to Early Adulthood: A Structural Magnetic Resonance Imaging Study", PLoS One 10, no. 3 (2015).

Harvard University, "Brain Architecture", *Center on the Developing Child*, [web article], https://developingchild.harvard.edu/science/key-concepts/brain-architecture/, (accessed 2 July 2018).

T. Payne Bryson and D. Siegel, *The Whole-Brain Child: 12 Proven Strategies to Nurture Your Child's Developing Mind*, London, Robinson, 2012.

028–029 MILESTONES: 2–3 YEARS
A. S. Dekaban and D. Sadowsky, "Changes in brain weights during the span of human life: relation of brain weights to body heights and body weights", *Annals of Neurology* 4, no. 4 (1978), pp345–356.

E. Hoff, "Language Experience and Language Milestones During Early Childhood", in K. McCartney and D. Phillips, (eds), *Blackwell Handbook of Early Childhood Development*, Blackwell Publishing, 2005, pp233–251.

S. P. Shelov and T. Remer Altmann (eds), *Caring for Your Baby and Young Child*, 5th ed., Itasca (IL), American Academy of Pediatrics, 2009, cited in American Academy of Pediatrics, "Language Development: 2 Year Olds", *Healthy Children*, [web article], 1 August 2009, https://www.healthychildren.org/English/ages-stages/toddler/Pages/Language-Development-2-Year-Olds.aspx, (accessed 2 July 2018).

032–033 MILESTONES 6–7 YEARS
V. S. Caviness Jr et al., "The human brain age 7-11 years: a volumetric analysis based on magnetic resonance images", *Cerebral Cortex* 6, no. 5 (1996), pp726–736.

J. Piaget, *The Essential Piaget*, H. E. Gruber and J. J. Vonèche (eds), New York, Basic Books, 1977.

036–037 THAT'S MINE
S. F. Warren, A. Rogers-Warren and D. M. Baer, "The role of offer rates in controlling sharing by young children", *Journal of Applied Behaviour Analysis* 9, no. 4 (1976), pp491–497.

N. Chernyak and T. Kushnir, "Giving pre-schoolers choice increases sharing behaviour", *Psychological Science* 24, no. 10 (2013), pp1971–1979.

J. H. Bryan and P. London, "Altruistic behaviour in children", *Psychological Bulletin* 73, no. 3 (1970), pp200–211.

046–047 BLUE CUP! NO, YELLOW CUP! NO, BLUE CUP!
B. Schwartz, *The Paradox of Choice: Why More is Less*, New York, Ecco, 2004.

H. A. Simon, "Rational choice and the structure of the environment", *Psychological Review* 63, no. 2 (1956), pp129–138.

050–051 NO COAT!
J. P. Owen et al., "Abnormal white matter microstructure in children with sensory processing disorders", *NeuroImage: Clinical*, no. 2 (2013), pp844–853, cited in J. Bunim, "Breakthrough Study Reveals Biological Basis for Sensory Processing Disorders in Kids", UCSF [web article], 9 July 2013, https://www.ucsf.edu/news/2013/07/107316/breakthrough-study-reveals-biological-basis-sensory-processing-disorders-kidsi, (accessed 27 June 2018).

S. Heller, *Too Loud, Too Bright, Too Fast, Too Tight: What to do if you are sensory defensive in an over-stimulating world*, New York, Harper Collins, 2003.

A. J. Ayres, *Sensory Integration and the Child: Understanding Hidden Sensory Challenges*, Los Angeles, Western Psychological Services, 2005.

056–057 WANT YOUR PHONE
A. Blum-Ross and S. Livingstone, "Families and screen time: current advice and emerging research", Media Policy Brief 17, London, Media Policy Project, London School of Economics and Political Science, 2016.

S. Livingstone et al., "Children's online activities, risks and safety: A literature review by the UKCCIS Evidence Group", UK Council for Child Internet Safety (UKCCIS), 2017.

058–059 JUST ONE MORE
A. K. Ventura and J. A. Mennella, "Innate and learned preferences for sweet taste during childhood", *Current Opinion in Clinical Nutrition & Metabolic Care* 14, no. 4 (2011), pp379–384, cited in G. C. Kroen, "Kids' Sugar Cravings Might Be Biological", NPR, [web article], 26 September 2011, https://www.npr.org/sections/thesalt/2011/09/26/140753048/kids-sugar-cravings-might-be-biological, (accessed 27 June 2018).

J. O. Fisher and L. L. Birch, "Eating in the absence of hunger and overweight in girls from 5 to 7 y of age", *American Journal of Clinical Nutrition* 76, no. 1 (2002), pp226–231.

062–063 SHYNESS
J. Kagan, J. S. Reznick and N. C. Snidman, "Biological Bases of Childhood Shyness", *Science* 240, no. 4849 (1988), pp167–171.

S. Cain, *Quiet: The Power of Introverts in a World That Can't Stop Talking*, London, Penguin, 2013.

066–067 I WANT IT NOW
W. Mischel, Y. Shoda and M. I. Rodriguez, "Delay of gratification in children", *Science* 244, no. 4907 (1989), pp933–938.

076–077 WANT THIS STORY
A. Shahaeian, et al. "Early shared reading, socioeconomic status, and children's cognitive and school competencies. *Scientific Studies of Reading* 22, no. 6 (2018): pp485–502.

M. Sénéchal and J. A. LeFevre, "Parental involvement in the development of children's reading skill: a five-year longitudinal study", *Child Development* 73, no. 2 (2002), pp445–460.

D. C. Kidd and E. Castano, "Reading Literary Fiction Improves Theory of Mind", *Science* 342, no. 6156 (2013), pp377-380.

J. S. Horst "Context and repetition in word learning", *Frontiers in Psychology* 4 (2013), p149.

078–079 I LIKE THIS STICK
G. Bento and G. Dias, "The importance of outdoor play for young children's healthy development", *Porto Biomedical Journal* 2, no. 5 (2017), pp157–160.

080–081 WHAT DOES THIS ONE DO?
C. Kidd and B. Y. Hayden, "The psychology and neuroscience of curiosity", *Neuron* 88, no. 3 (2015), pp449–460.

P. Y. Oudeyer and L. B. Smith, "How Evolution May Work Through Curiosity-Driven Developmental Process", *Topics in Cognitive Science* 8, no. 2 (2016), pp492–502.

S. Engel, *The Hungry Mind: The Origins of Curiosity in Childhood*, Cambridge (MA), Harvard University Press, 2018 (reprint edition).

J. Panksepp, *Affective Neuroscience: The*

Foundations of Human and Animal Emotions, Oxford, Oxford University Press, 1998.

M. Sunderland, *The Science of Parenting*, London, Dorling Kindersley, 2008.

084–085 CARVING OUT QUALITY TIME
D. Elkind, *The Hurried Child: Growing Up Too Fast Too Soon*, Cambridge (MA), Perseus Publishing, 2001.

M. Sunderland, "The science behind how holidays make your child happier – and smarter", *The Telegraph*, [web article], 1 February 2017, https://www.telegraph.co.uk/travel/family-holidays/the-science-behind-how-holidays-make-your-child-happier-and-smarter/, (accessed 28 June 2018).

S. M. Siviy and J. Panksepp, "In search of the neurobiological substrates for social playfulness in mammalian brains", *Neuroscience and Biobehavioural Reviews* 35, no. 9 (2011), pp1821–1830.

086–087 WHEN IS TOMORROW?
P. J. Bauer and T. Pathman, "Memory and Early Brain Development", in R. E. Tremblay, M. Boivin and R. D. V. Peters (eds), *Encyclopedia on Early Childhood Development* [online], December 2008, http://www.child-encyclopedia.com/brain/according-experts/memory-and-early-brain-development, [accessed 28 June 2018].

S. J. Beneke, M. M. Ostrosky and L. G. Katz, "Calendar time for young children: Good intentions gone awry", *Young Children* 63, no. 3 (2008), pp12–16.

K. A. Tillman and D. Barner, "Learning the language of time: Children's acquisition of duration words", *Cognitive Psychology* 78 (2015), pp55–77.

G. Burton and D. Edge, "Helping Children Develop a Concept of Time", *School Science and Mathematics* 85, no. 2 (1985), pp109–120.

090–091 I WANT A CUDDLE
J. Kagan, "The Biography of Behavioral Inhibition", in M. Zentner and R. L. Shiner, (eds), *Handbook of Temperament*, Guilford Press, 2012, pp69–82.

094–095 I WANT MY DUMMY!
E. Bachar et al., "Childhood vs. Adolescence Transitional Object Attachment, and Its Relation to Mental Health and Parental Bonding", *Child Psychiatry and Human Development* 28, no. 3 (1998), pp149–167.

D. W. Winnicott, "Transitional Objects and Transitional Phenomena – A Study of the First Not-Me Possession", *The International Journal of Psychoanalysis* 34 (1953), pp89–97.

NHS, "Sweets, fizzy drinks and bottles", NHS [web article], 25 November 2015,

https://www.nhs.uk/Livewell/dentalhealth/Pages/Goodhabitskids.aspx, (accessed 28 June 2018).

096–097 ARE YOU SAD, MUMMY
D. Goleman, *Emotional Intelligence: Why it can matter more than IQ*, London, Bloomsbury, 1996.

098–099 I'M GOING TO EXPLODE
R. W. Greene, *The Explosive Child: A New Approach for Understanding and Parenting Easily Frustrated, Chronically Inflexible Children*, 5th ed., New York, Harper Paperbacks, 2014.

S. Shanker, *Self-Reg: How to Help Your Child (and You) Break the Stress Cycle and Successfully Engage with Life*, London, Penguin, 2017 (reprint edition).

100–101 I'M JUST GOING TO DO IT
T. Payne Bryson and D. Siegel, *The Whole-Brain Child: 12 Proven Strategies to Nurture Your Child's Developing Mind*, London, Robinson, 2012.

102–103 THAT'S SO FUNNY
A. S. Honig, "Research in Review: Humor Development in Children", *Young Children* 43, no. 4 (1988), pp16–73.

C. Lyon, "Humour and the young child: A review of the research literature", *TelevIZIon* 19 (2006), pp4–9.

104–105 CAN MR GIRAFFE SIT DOWN TOO?
M. Taylor, *Imaginary Companions and the Children Who Create Them*, Oxford, Oxford University Press, 1999.

M. Taylor and C.M. Mottweiler, "Imaginary companions: Pretending they are real but knowing they are not", *American Journal of Play* 1 (2008), pp47–54.

108–109 I LOVE BEING WITH YOU
J. Bowlby, *The Making and Breaking of Affectional Bonds*, Abingdon, Routledge, 2005.

M. Sunderland, *The Science of Parenting*, London, Dorling Kindersley, 2008.

110–111 WHY IS THE SKY BLUE?
M. M. Chouinard, "Children's questions: a mechanism for cognitive development", *Monogr Soc Res Child Dev.* 72, no. 1 (2007), pp1–112.

A. Gopnik, A. Meltzoff and P. K. Kuhl, *The Scientist in the Crib: Minds, Brains and How Children Learn*, New York, William Morrow, 1999.

E. Elsworthy, "Curious children ask 73 questions each day – many of which parents can't answer, says study", *The Independent*, [web article], 3 December 2017, https://www.independent.co.uk/news/uk/home-news/curious-children-questions-parenting-mum-dad-google-answers-inquisitive-argos-toddlers-chad-

valley-a8089821.html, (accessed 28 June 2018).

B. A. Goldfield, "Vocabulary Size in the First Language", in C. A. Chapelle (ed.), *The Encyclopedia of Applied Linguistics*, Hoboken, Wiley-Blackwell, 2012.

B. N. Frazier, S. A. Gelman and H. M. Wellman, "Preschoolers' search for explanatory information within adult-child conversation", *Child Development* 80, no. 6 (2009), pp1592–1611.

114–115 WHEN I WAS LITTLE...
C. M. Alberini and A. Travaglia, "Infantile Amnesia: A Critical Period of Learning to Learn and Remember", *The Journal of Neuroscience* 37, no. 24 (2017), pp5783–5795.

D. Amso, "When Do Children Start Making Long-Term Memories?", *Scientific American*, [web article], 1 January 2017, https://www.scientificamerican.com/article/when-do-children-start-making-long-term-memories/, (accessed 2 July 2018).

116–117 I GIVE UP
C. Dweck, *Mindset: Changing The Way You Think To Fulfil Your Potential*, London, Robinson, 2017 (revised edition).

M. Hill et al., "Parenting and resilience", [booklet], Joseph Rowntree Foundation, 2007.

K. R. Ginsburg, *Building Resilience in Children and Teens: Giving Kids Roots and Wings*, 2nd ed., Itasca (IL), American Academy of Pediatrics, 2011.

126–127 I'VE LOST TEDDY
C. J. Litt, "Theories of Transitional Object Attachment: An Overview", *International Journal of Behavioral Development* 9, no. 3 (1986), pp383–399.

D. W. Winnicott, "Transitional Objects and Transitional Phenomena – A Study of the First Not-Me Possession", *The International Journal of Psychoanalysis* 34 (1953), pp89–97.

128–129 YOU'RE ALWAYS TOO BUSY
D. Elkind, *The Hurried Child: Growing Up Too Fast Too Soon*, Cambridge (MA), Perseus Publishing, 2001.

D. Code, *Kids Pick Up on Everything: How Parental Stress is Toxic to Kids*, Createspace, 2011.

K. Salmela-Aro, L. Tynkkynen, and J. Vuori, "Parents' work burnout and adolescents' school burnout: Are they shared?", *European Journal of Developmental Psychology* 8, no. 2 (2011), pp215–227.

130–131 I HATE HER
A. Faber and E. Mazlish, *Siblings Without Rivalry: How to Help Your Children Live Together So You Can Live Too*, New York, W. W. Norton & Company, 2012.

132–133 I FEEL SAD
T. Payne Bryson and D. Siegel, *The Whole-Brain Child: 12 Proven Strategies to Nurture Your Child's Developing Mind*, London, Robinson, 2012.

136–137 DEALING WITH A POORLY CHILD
E. Barlow, "Three Million Working Days Are Lost Each Year To Care For Sick Children", *Female First*, [web article], 4 December 2015, http://www.femalefirst.co.uk/parenting/three-million-working-days-year-care-sick-children-900451.html, (accessed 2 July 2018).

C. Eiser, "Changes in understanding of illness as the child grows", *Archives of Disease in Childhood* 60 (1985), pp489–492.

138–139 THEY SAY I'M A CRY BABY
E. Kennedy-Moore, "Helping Children Who Cry Easily", *Psychology Today*, [web article], 1 September 2013, https://www.psychologytoday.com/us/blog/growing-friendships/201308/helping-children-who-cry-easily, (accessed 2 July 2018).

E. N. Aron, *The Highly Sensitive Child: Helping Our Children Thrive When the World Overwhelms Them*, New York, Harmony, 2002.

D. J. Kindlon, *Raising Cain: Protecting the Emotional Life of Boys*, New York, Ballantine Books, 2000.

140–141 I'VE HAD A BAD DREAM
A. S. Honig and A. L. Nealis, "What do young children dream about?", *Early Child Development and Care* 182, no. 6 (2012), pp771–795.

J. D. Woolley and H. M. Wellman, "Children's concept of dreams", *Cognitive Development* 7, no. 3 (1992), pp365–380.

T. A. Nielsen et al., "Development of disturbing dreams during adolescence and their relation to anxiety symptoms", *Sleep* 23, no. 6 (2000), pp1–10, cited in P. McNamara, "Children's Dreams and Nightmares", *Psychology Today*, [web article], 30 October 2016, https://www.psychologytoday.com/gb/blog/dream-catcher/201610/childrens-dreams-and-nightmares, (accessed 27 June 2018).

144–145 I'VE HAD AN ACCIDENT
M. Wells and L. Bonner, *Effective Management of Bladder and Bowel Problems in Children*, London, Class Publishing, 2008, cited in "Children who soil or wet themselves: information for parents, carers and anyone who works with children", leaflet, Royal College of Psychiatrists, https://www.rcpsych.ac.uk/healthadvice/parentsandyoungpeople/parentscarers/soilingorwetting.aspx, (accessed online 28 June 2018).

146–146 SHE'S SO ANNOYING
M. Thompson, *Mom, They're Teasing Me: Helping Your Child Solve Social Problems*, New York, Ballantine Books, 2002.

150–151 YOU HAVE TO
M. Thompson, *Mom, They're Teasing Me: Helping Your Child Solve Social Problems*, New York, Ballantine Books, 2002.

154–155 BIRTHDAY PARTIES
Asda/The Telegraph, "Parents spend £19k on children's birthday parties over lifetime", *The Telegraph*, [web article], 25 May 2015, https://www.telegraph.co.uk/news/shopping-and-consumer-news/11627237/Parents-spend-19k-on-childrens-birthday-parties-over-lifetime.html, (accessed 28 June 2018).

J. Woolley, "The All-Important Annual Birthday Party", *Psychology Today*, [web article], 10 January 2013, https://www.psychologytoday.com/us/blog/what-children-know/201301/the-all-important-annual-birthday-party, (accessed 28 June 2018).

158–159 I WET THE BED
NHS, "Bedwetting in under-5s", *NHS* [web article], 8 October 2015, https://www.nhs.uk/conditions/pregnancy-and-baby/bedwetting/, (accessed 27 June 2018).

National Institute for Health and Clinical Excellence, *Nocturnal enuresis: The management of bedwetting in children and young people*, London, National Clinical Guideline Centre, 2010.

Canadian Paediatric Society, "Bedwetting (enuresis)", *Paediatrics & Child Health* 3, no. 2 (1998), p141.

164–165 HAVE I MADE YOU SAD?
T. Carey, *Taming the Tiger Parent: How to put your child's well-being first in a competitive world*, London, Robinson, 2014.

170–171 SEPARATION AND DIVORCE
H. Westberg, T. S. Nelson, and K. W. Piercy, "Disclosure of Divorce Plans to Children: What the Children Have to Say", *Contemporary Family Therapy* 24, no. 4 (2002), pp525–542.

J. Healy, A. Stewart, and A. Copeland, "The Role of Self-Blame in Children's Adjustment to Parental Separation", *Personality and Social Psychology Bulletin* 19, no. 3, pp279–289.

174–175 NO COLOURING ON THE WALL
L. E. Berk, *Infants, Children, and Adolescents*, 4th Ed, Boston, Allyn & Bacon, 2002.

182–183 I CAN'T DO IT
T. E. Chansky, *Freeing Your Child from Negative Thinking: Powerful, Practical Strategies to Build a Lifetime of Resilience, Flexibility, and Happiness*, Cambridge (MA), Da Capo Lifelong Books, 2008.

T. Carey, *Taming the Tiger Parent: How to put your child's well-being first in a competitive world*, London, Robinson, 2014.

188–189 GOOD MANNERS
D. Auerbach, "Could your manners impact your career?", *CareerBuilder*, [web article], 27 August 2014, https://www.careerbuilder.com/advice/could-your-manners-impact-your-career, (accessed 28 June 2018).

M. Thompson, *Mom, They're Teasing Me: Helping Your Child Solve Social Problems*, New York, Ballantine Books, 2002.

E. Cook and R. Dunifron, "Do Family Meals Really Make a Difference?", Parenting in Context, Cornell University College of Human Ecology, 2012.

190–191 NO ONE LIKES ME
J. Mize and G. S. Pettit, "Mothers' social coaching, mother-child relationship style, and children's peer competence: is the medium the message?", *Child Development* 68, no. 2 (1997), pp312–332.

E. Kennedy-Moore and C. McLaughlin, *Growing Friendships. A Kids' Guide to Making and Keeping Friends*, Hillsboro, Beyond Words Publishing, 2017.

M. Thompson, *Mom, They're Teasing Me: Helping Your Child to Solve Social Problems*, New York, Ballantine Books, 2002.

E. Kennedy-Moore, "What Are Social Skills? Helping children become comfortable and competent in social situations", *Psychology Today*, [web article], 18 August 2011, https://www.psychologytoday.com/intl/blog/growing-friendships/201108/what-are-social-skills, (accessed 27 June 2018).

T. Carey, "Does your child struggle to make friends? They could be suffering from social dyslexia", *The Telegraph*, [web article], 31 August 2016, https://www.telegraph.co.uk/women/family/does-your-child-struggle-to-make-friends-they-could-be-suffering/, (accessed 27 June 2018).

196–197 I DON'T WANT TO GO TO SCHOOL
L. Wilmshurst, *Clinical and Educational Child Psychology. An Ecological-Transnational Approach to Understanding Child Problems and Interventions*, Hoboken, Wiley-Blackwell, 2013.

200–201 SCHOOL PRESSURE
H. Gardner, *Frames of Mind: The Theory of Multiple Intelligences*, New York, Basic Books, 1983.

H. Gardner, *Multiple Intelligences: New Horizons in Theory and Practice*, New York, Basic Books, 2006.

P. Tough, *How Children Succeed*, New York, Random House Books, 2013.

T. Carey, *Taming the Tiger Parent: How to put your child's well-being first in a competitive world*, London, Robinson, 2014.

204–205 I'M THE BEST
E. Brummelman and S. Thomaes, "How Children Construct Views of Themselves: A Social-Developmental Perspective", *Child Development* 88, no. 6 (2017), pp1763–1773.

E. Brummelman et al., "Origins of narcissism in children", *Proceedings of the National Academy of Sciences* 112, no. 12 (2015), pp3659–3662.

208–209 BUT ALL MY FRIENDS HAVE ONE
L. N. Chaplin and D. R. John, "Growing up in a Material World: Age Differences in Materialism in Children and Adolescents", *Journal of Consumer Research* 34, no. 4 (2007), pp480–493.

J. B. Schor, *Born to Buy: The Commercialized Child and the New Consumer Culture*, New York, Simon & Schuster, 2004.

212–213 MONEY MATTERS
A. Bucciol and M. Veronesi, "Teaching Children to Save and Lifetime Savings: What is the Best Strategy?", *Journal of Economic Psychology* 45 (2013), pp1–17.

A. Furnham, "The saving and spending habits of young people", *Journal of Forensic Psychology* 20 (1999), pp677–697.

R. Rubin, "Kids vs. Teens: Money and Maturity Guide to Online Behaviour", eMarket, 2004.

P. Webley, R. M. Levine, and A. Lewis, "A study in economic psychology: Children's saving in a play economy", in S. Maital and S. Maital (eds), *Economics and Psychology*, Edward Elgar, 1993, pp61–80.

A. Strauss and K. Schuessler, "Socialization, logical reasoning and concept development in the child", *American Sociological Review* 16 (1951), pp514–523.

A. F. Furnham, "Parental attitudes towards pocket money/allowances for children", *Journal of Economic Psychology* 22 (2001), pp397–422.

214–215 STOP FIGHTING!
M. El-Sheikh, E. M. Cummings, and S. Reiter, "Preschoolers' responses to ongoing interadult conflict: The role of prior exposure to resolved versus unresolved arguments", *Journal of Abnormal Child Psychology* 24, no. 5 (1996), pp665–679.

M. El-Sheikh, "Children's responses to adult–adult and mother–child arguments: The role of parental marital conflict and distress", *Journal of Family Psychology* 11, no. 2 (1997), pp165–175.

A. M. Graham, P. A. Fisher, and J. H. Pfeifer, "What Sleeping Babies Hear: An fMRI Study of Interparental Conflict and Infants' Emotion Processing", *Psychological Science* 24, no. 5 (2013), pp782–789.

216–217 BUT I'M NOT TIRED
Stanford Children's Health, "Sleep and Your Child", *Stanford Children's*, [web article], http://www.stanfordchildrens.org/en/topic/default?id=sleep-and-your-child-1-2909, (accessed 2 July 2018).

M. Wood, "Electronic devices, kids and sleep: How screen time keeps them awake", *Science Life (The University of Chicago Medicine)*, [web article], 17 February 2016, https://sciencelife.uchospitals.edu/2016/02/17/electronic-devices-kids-and-sleep-how-screen-time-keeps-them-awake/, (accessed 2 July 2018).

218–219 I'M BORED
S. Mann and R. Cadman, "Does Being Bored Make Us More Creative?", *Creativity Research Journal* 26, no. 2 (2014), pp165–173, cited in British Psychological Society (BPS), "Boredom can be good for you, scientists say", *ScienceDaily* [web article], 24 March 2015, www.sciencedaily.com/releases/2015/03/150324205940.htm, (accessed 25 June 2018).

E. Rhodes, "The exciting side of boredom", *The Psychologist* 28, no. 4 (2015), pp278–281.

A. D. Pellegrini and C. M. Bohn-Gettler, "The Benefits of Recess in Primary School", *Scholarpedia* 8, no. 2 (2013), p30448.

D. G. Singer et al., "Children's Pastimes and Play in Sixteen Nations: Is Free-Play Declining?", *American Journal of Play* 1, no. 3 (2009), pp283–312.

A. A. Brooks, *Children of Fast-Track Parents*, New York, Viking Books, 1989.

222–223 I'VE GOT A BOYFRIEND
R. P. Carlisle, *Encyclopedia of Play in Today's Society*, vol. 1, Thousand Oaks, SAGE Publications, 2009.

224–225 I'M NOT PLAYING ANY MORE!
B. Priewasser, J. Roessler, and J. Perner, "Competition as rational action: why young children cannot appreciate competitive games", *Journal of Experimental Child Psychology* 116, no. 2 (2013), pp545–559.

230–231 DO I HAVE TO DO MUSIC PRACTICE?
C. Chau and T. Riforgiate, "The Influence of Music on the Development of Children", BSc project, California Polytechnic State University, San Luis Obispo, 2010.

B. M. McGarity, "Relationships among Cognitive Processing Styles, Musical Ability and Language Ability", MEd thesis, University of New England, New South Wales, 1986.

232–233 WHAT'S A STRANGER?
"Staying safe away from home", *NSPCC*, [web article], https://www.nspcc.org.uk/preventing-abuse/keeping-children-safe/staying-safe-away-from-home/, (accessed 2 July 2018).

234–235 MY DIARY – KEEP OUT
H. M. Gordon, T. D. Lyon, and K. Lee, "Social and cognitive factors associated with children's secret-keeping for a parent", *Child Development* 85, no. 6 (2014), pp2374–2388.

M. D. Griffiths, "Writing Wrongs: Diary writing and psychological wellbeing", *Psychology Today*, [web article], 14 July 2015, https://www.psychologytoday.com/us/blog/in-excess/201507/writing-wrongs, (accessed 2 July 2018).

K. Klein and A. Boals, "Expressive writing can increase working memory capacity", *Journal of Experimental Psychology: General* 130 no. 3 (2001), pp520–533.

M. D. Lieberman et al., "Putting Feelings Into Words: Affect Labeling Disrupts Amygdala Activity in Response to Afferctive Stimuli", *Psychological Science* 18, no. 5 (2007), pp421–428, cited in I. Sample, "Keeping a diary makes you happier", *The Guardian*, [web article], 15 February 2009, http://www.guardian.co.uk/science/2009/feb/15/psychology-usa, (accessed 2 July 2018).

236–237 WHY DO YOU HAVE TO GO TO WORK?
D. Elkind, *The Hurried Child: Growing Up Too Fast Too Soon*, Cambridge (MA), Perseus Publishing, 2001.

240–241 I WANT A PHONE
S. Livingstone et al., "Children's online activities, risks and safety: A literature review by the UKCCIS Evidence Group", UK Council for Child Internet Safety (UKCCIS), 2017.

K. M. Collier et al., "Does parental mediation of media influence child outcomes? A meta-analysis on media time, aggression, substance use, and sexual behavior", *Developmental Psychology* 52, no. 5 (2016), pp798–812.

242–243 I'M NOT PRETTY ENOUGH
L. Papadopoulos, *Sexualisation of Young People Review*, UK Home Office, 2010.

244–245 AFTER-SCHOOL ACTIVITIES
J. Hamilton, "Scientists Say Child's Play Helps Build A Better Brain", NPR, [web article], 6 August 2014, https://www.npr.org/sections/ed/2014/08/06/336361277/scientists-say-childs-play-helps-build-a-better-brain, (accessed 28 June 2018).

A. D. Pellegrini and C. M. Bohn-Gettler, "The Benefits of Recess in Primary School", *Scholarpedia* 8, no. 2 (2013), p30448.

D. Elkins, "Are We Pushing Our Kids Too Hard?", *Psychology Today*, [web article], 1 January 2003, https://www.psychologytoday.com/gb/articles/200303/are-we-pushing-our-kids-too-hard, (accessed 28 June 2018).

A. A. Brooks, *Children of Fast-Track Parents*, New York, Viking Books, 1989.

Index

A

abduction, fear of 232, 233
accidents, toilet 144–45
achievements, comparison of 204
activities 85, 244–45
adrenaline 25
affection, parents' experience of 15
after-school activities 244–45
age restrictions 227
aggression, hitting and biting 54–55
agility 31
amnesia, infantile 114
amygdala 19, 26, 61
anger
    4–5-year-olds 31, 98–99
    6–7-year-olds 184–85, 214–15
    parents arguing 171, 214–15
anxiety
    bedwetting 159
    helicopter parenting 239
    fear of the dark 118–19
    lack of confidence 182–83
    school 196–97
    strangers 232–33
    terrorist attacks 160–61
appearance 242–43
appetite 59
approval, craving 164–65
assertiveness 48–49
attachment
    attachment play 84
    to dummies 94–95
    night times 74
    secure attachment 108–109
    separation anxiety 52–53, 61, 63, 74, 90–91
    to toys 126–27
attention
    attention-seeking behaviour 84
    attention span 30, 203
    attentive parenting 18
    negative attention 71
    positive attention 55, 92–93, 189
    selective attention 194–95
    undivided attention 128–29
autonomic nervous system 18

B

bad dreams 140–41
balance 29, 31

Beavers 244
bedtimes 74–75, 84
    2–3-year-olds 75, 76–7
    4–5-year-olds 75, 119, 141, 159
    6–7-year-olds 75, 85, 216–17
    older children 180–81
    parents' experience of 14
    staggered bedtimes 85
    story time 76–77
bedwetting 144, 158–59, 171
behaviour, praising good 45
birthday parties 152–55
biting 54–55, 156
board games 83, 189, 191, 225
boasting 204–205
body awareness 33
body image 242–43
body language, illness and 137
bonds, improving 84–85
books 76–77, 107
boredom 218–19
bossiness 48–49, 150–51
boundaries 101
    4–5-year-olds 31, 127, 174–75, 136
    6–7-year-olds 239
    illness and 136
    independence and 239
    special toys and 127
    testing 31, 174–75
boyfriends 222–23
brain development 8, 24–27
    2–3-year-olds 28, 79
    4–5-year-olds 30, 114
    6–7-year-olds 32
    how children learn 24–25
    infantile amnesia and 114
brave talk 61, 91, 136
breathing, crying and 139
bribes, fussy eaters and 43
Brownies 244
buffer time 79
bullying 192

C

cafés, family friendly 44
calmness 156
    dealing with temper tantrums 41
    dummies and 95
    illnesses and 136
    waiting for 19
capabilities 29

car journeys 122–23
cause and effect
    2–3-year-olds 28, 70, 81
    4–5-year-olds 133, 155, 175
celebrity culture 243
cerebral cortex 26
child-centred parenting 18–19
childcare 106
    2–3-year-olds 52–53, 60–61
    childminders 60–61
childhood, parents' experience of 14–15
choice 46–47, 51
clearing up 148–49
clinginess
    2–3-year-olds 52–53, 63
    4–5-year-olds 90–91
    see also separation anxiety
clothes 50–51
co-parenting
    parenting mission statement 16
    parenting style conflicts 15, 186–87
cognitive development
    2–3-year-olds 79, 56–57, 64–65
    4–5-year-olds 92–93
    phones and 56–57
    pretend play 64–65
comforters
    dummies 94–95
    food as 59
commitments, honouring 168–69
communication, open and honest 21
comparison to others 30, 33, 173
compassion 211
competitive behaviour
    4–5-year-olds 165
    6–7-year-olds 32, 224–25
    competitive parenting 201
computers 129
    video games 119, 141, 216–17
    websites 226–27
concentration 30, 32
confidence
    2–3-year-olds 39, 48, 61, 72
    4–5-year-olds 93, 114
    6–7-year-olds 182–83, 193, 205
    anxieties about lack of 182–83
    boosting and reaffirming 61, 114
    building parenting confidence 20–21
    self-confidence 193
    undermining 39
conflict
    dealing with 124–25

friendships 192–93
parenting style 186–7
parents' own experience of 14
peer conflict 146–47, 155
sibling relationships and rivalry 124–25, 130–31, 134–35
consequences, learning about 51
control, feelings of 31
conversation skills 30, 111
cooperation 112–13, 189
coordination
2–3-year-olds 29, 45
4–5-year-olds 31
6–7-year-olds 230
coping skills and strategies 116, 139
corpus callosum 27
cortisol 25, 211
courtesy 188–89
creativity 200, 218
crib-sheet, parenting 18–19
criticism, self- 211
crying 96–97, 138–39
Cubs 244
cuddles
2–3-year-olds 85
4–5-year-olds 90–91, 109, 137, 161, 171
illness and 137
cues
sleep cues 75
social cues 53, 136, 190, 192
curiosity
2–3-year-olds 64, 80–81
4–5-year-olds 101, 110–11, 162–63
about genitals 162–63

D

dark, fear of the 118–19
death 166–67
decision making 46–47, 50–51
defiance 31
delaying tactics, avoiding 93
demanding children 48–49
development, how children learn 24–25
developmental stages 10
2–3-year-olds 28–29, 34–87
4–5-year-olds 30–31, 88–175
6–7-year-olds 32–33, 176–243
devices
2–3-year-olds 56–57
4–5-year-olds 129, 169
6–7-year-olds 208–209, 216–17, 226–28, 240–41
car journeys 122
phones 45, 56–57, 169, 240–41
quality time and 85
dexterity 31

diaries 234–35
disappointment, managing 168–69
discipline
lying and 143
parents' own experience of 14
using shame to 211
distractions 21
gratification delay 67
impatience and 87
self-touching and 163
separation anxiety and 53
divorce 170–71
dopamine 25, 80
downtime 245
drawing skills 29, 31, 174–75
dreams, bad 140–41
drinks 145
dummies 94–95

E

eating out 44–45
effort, praising 200, 221
egocentricity 29
electronic nannies 227
embarrassing parents 206–207
emotions 235
2–3-year-olds 28, 29, 59, 77
4–5-year-olds 31, 92–93, 96–97, 132–33, 139, 156–57
6–7-year-olds 184–85, 193, 200, 215, 230–31
acknowledging negative 19
boys and 139
brain development and 26, 27
developing emotional intelligence 96–97
emotional understanding 77
emotional wellbeing 18–19, 193, 200
learning about 25
linking food with 59
music lessons 230–31
positive emotions 97
regulating 156–57
using conflict to teach about 215
see also individual emotions
empathy 18
2–3-year-olds 62, 82
4–5-year-olds 31, 96, 131, 152
6–7-year-olds 191
emotional intelligence and 96
sharing and 82
shyness and 62
exercise 245
expectations 143
exploration 78–79
expression, storytelling and 77
externalizing 197

eye contact 189
2–3-year-olds 41
4–5-year-olds 99, 109, 113
6–7-year-olds 85, 191

F

fairness, sense of 168, 180–81
family meetings 125
family time 236–37
favouritism 124–25
fears
4–5-year-olds 98, 118–19, 160–61
6–7-year-olds 208–209
anger and 98
fear of the dark 118–19
fear of missing out 208–209
of terrorist attacks 160–61
feelings
2–3-year-olds 29, 61
4–5-year-olds 31, 109, 132–33
6–7-year-olds 32, 33, 234–35
acknowledging 61
contradictory 31
diaries and 234–35
learning about 25
parents' expression of 15
positive 109
fight-or-flight response 19, 26
2–3-year-olds 55, 71
4–5-year-olds 101, 113
6–7-year-olds 182, 214
parents' instinct 156
fighting
play-fighting 55
sibling rivalry 124, 125
films 119, 141
fine motor skills
2–3-year-olds 29
4–5-year-olds 31
6–7-year-olds 33
5-year-old development see 4–5-year-old development
FOMO (fear of missing out) 244
food
2–3-year-olds 42–43, 58–59
fussy eaters 42–43
playing with food 43
portion sizes 43
sweet food 58–59
4–5-year-old development 10, 88–175
after-school activities 245
anger 98–99
asserting independence 156–57
bad dreams 140–41
bedwetting 158–59
birthday parties 152–53, 155
bossiness 150–51

car journeys 123
carving out quality time 85, 109, 135
craving approval 164–65
crying 138–39
cuddles 90–91, 109
curiosity 101, 110–11
curiosity about genitals 162–63
daytime wetting 144–45
dealing with death 166–67
dummies 94–95
eating out 45
emotional intelligence 96–97
fears 118–19
fears of terrorist attacks 160–61
friendships 150–53
good manners 189
hitting and biting 55
humour and laughter 102–103
imaginary friends 104–105
keeping promises 168–69
lying and honesty 142–43
memories 114–15
milestones 30–31
money 212–13
moving home 107
need for recognition 92–93
new additions to the family 134–35
peer conflict 146–47
perfectionism 172–73
poorly children 137
quality time 128–29
questions and curiosity 110–11
resilience 116–17
sadness 132–33
school pressure 201
secure attachments 108–109
seeking cooperation 112–13
self-control 100–101
separation anxiety 90–91
separation and divorce 171
shyness 63, 91
sibling relationships and rivalry
  124–25, 130–31, 134–35
sleep 75
special toys 126–27
tale-telling 120–21
technology 227
testing boundaries 174–75
tidying up 148–49
friendships
  2–3-year-olds 77
  4–5-year-olds 30, 104–105, 146–47,
    150–53, 155
  6–7-year-olds 32, 189, 190–93,
    198–99, 204–205, 222–25
  best friends 198–99
  birthday parties 152–53, 155
  boasting 204–205

bossiness 150–51
boyfriends and girlfriends 222–23
competitive behaviour 224–25
emotional understanding and 77
forming first 25
good manners and 189
imaginary friends 104–105
peer conflict 146–47, 155
peer pressure 32, 206, 207, 208,
  209, 216, 241
play dates 63, 105, 107, 150–51, 189,
  223, 241, 244, 245
sharing and 83
shyness and 63
frustration 41, 98, 184–85
fussy eaters 42–43

G

games
  board games 83, 189, 191, 225
  car journeys 123
  eating out 45
  pretend play 64–65
  sharing 83
  winning and losing 224–25
generosity 200
genitals, curiosity about 162–63
girlfriends 222–23
"good enough" parenting 20–21
gratification delay
  2–3-year-olds 66–67, 87
  6–7-year-olds 179, 212
grief 167
gross motor skills 33
growth 29
growth mindset 173
guilt
  about separation and divorce 170
  about working 236–37
  peer pressure 208

H

hand holding 108–109
hatred 19, 184–85
healthy bodies 243
helicopter parenting 239
help
  encouraging 85
  resisting 38–39
hitting 54–55, 156, 157
holidays 14, 84
homes, moving 106–107
homework
  4–5-year-olds 173
  6–7-year-olds 75, 182–83, 201,
    202–3, 226, 227

parents' own experience of 14
honesty 142–43
humour 49, 102–103
hunger 59
hydration 145

I

illnesses 136–37
  school and 196–97
imaginary friends 104–105
imagination
  2–3-year-olds 28, 57, 77
  4–5-year-olds 104, 118–19
  imaginary friends 104–105
impatience 86–87
impulse-control
  2–3-year-olds 66–67, 71
  4–5-year-olds 100–101
independence
  2–3-year-olds 38–39, 42–43,
    50–51, 69
  4–5-year-olds 156–57
  6–7-year-olds 33, 238–39
  food and 42–43
  play time and 69
infantile amnesia 114
inquisitive minds 80–81
intelligence, emotional 29, 96–97
internet 226–27
interrupting people 178–79
intervention 39
irony 103

J

jealousy 84, 124–25
joke telling 102–103

K

kicking 54, 156, 157
kindness 55, 152, 200

L

labelling, avoiding 62, 91
language development
  2–3-year-olds 28, 48–49
  4–5-year-olds 30, 103, 110, 114
  6–7-year-olds 32
  memories and 114
laughter 102–103
leadership 151
learning, how children learn
  24–25
limbic system 26, 29
logic 31, 32

losing and winning 224–25
lying 142–43

M

make-believe 64–65
manners 44, 49, 188–89
  table manners 43, 45, 188
manual dexterity 31
map reading 123
material possessions, own experience of 15
mealtimes
  2–3-year-olds 42–45, 59
  6–7-year-olds 188
  eating out 44–45
  fussy eaters 42–43
memories and memory development
  2–3-year-olds 28, 77
  4–5-year-olds 30, 114–15
  6–7-year-olds 33
mental brakes 100
milestones
  2–3 years 28–29
  4–5 years 30–31
  6–7 years 32–33
mindfulness
  mindful parenting 237
  mindful walking 79
misbehaviour 92
mistakes
  learning from 116
  making 210–11, 213
  perfectionism and 172–73
mobile phones
  2–3-year-olds 45, 56–57, 85
  4–5-year-olds 122, 129, 169
  6–7-year-olds 226, 240–41
  car journeys 122
  quality time and 85
money 212–13
motion sickness 123
motivation 164–65, 220–21
mourning 167
movement, freedom of 29
moving house 106–107
muscle strength 31
music lessons 230–31

N

nagging 112–13, 178
nannies, electronic 227
naps 74, 75, 154
negativity 183
  acknowledging negative emotions 19
  negative attention 71
  negative self-talk 211, 221
night-lights 75, 119

night-time waking 74, 75
nightmares 140–41
numbers 32

O

object categorization 30
online activity 226–27
outdoor activities and play 79, 147
ownership, concept of 37
oxytocin 25

P

parents
  building confidence 20–21
  child's preference for one 72–73
  competitive parenting 201
  conflicts between 186–87, 214–15
  own experiences of childhood 14–15
  parenting mission statement 16
  pressure to be "perfect" 20–21
  as role models 18
  separation and divorce 170–71, 215
  values 16–17
patience 66–67, 122
peers
  peer conflict 146–47, 155
  peer pressure 32, 206, 207, 208,
    209, 216, 241
  see also friendships
pencils, holding 31
perfectionism 172–73, 211
  physical perfectionism 242–43
personal space 125
pester power 208–209
phones see mobile phones
physical affection, own experience
  of 15
physical perfectionism 242–43
physical skills 33, 79
pinching 54
planning 30, 33
play 244
  2–3-year-olds 55, 68–69, 72, 83, 84
  4–5-year-olds 104–105, 146–49
  6–7-year-olds 201, 203, 219, 245
  attachment play 84
  disrupting or ending 68–69
  free play 219, 245
  imaginary friends 104–105
  learning through 203
  outdoor play 147
  peer conflict 146–47
  play-fighting 55
  play islands 68
  rough-and-tumble 55, 72
  sharing games 83

tidying up 148–49
  see also games; play dates; role
    play; toys
play dates
  2–3-year-olds 63
  4–5-year-olds 105, 107
  6–7-year-olds 189, 223, 241, 244, 245
  bossiness and 150–51
pocket money 212–13
points of view 32
politeness 45, 49, 70, 188–89
poorly children 136–37
positivity
  positive attention 55, 92–93, 189
  positive emotions 97
  positive feelings 109
possessions, own experience of 15
power struggles 39, 51
praise
  decision making 47
  praising effort 200, 205, 221
  praising qualities 173, 205
  search for 92–93, 164–65
predictability 48, 49
prefrontal cortex 30
presents 155
pretend play 64–65
  imaginary friends 104–105
pride 33, 38, 164, 205
priorities 209
privacy 33, 234–35
problem solving
  2–3-year-olds 39, 64
  4–5-year-olds 116, 117
promises, keeping 168–69
pronunciation 28

Q

quality time 84–85
  4–5-year-olds 109, 125, 128–29, 135
  sibling rivalry and 125
questions and questioning
  2–3-year-olds 77, 80–81
  4–5-year-olds 30, 110–11

R

reading 32
reasoning 28
recall 28
recognition 92–93
refusals to do something 50–51
rejection
  feelings of 84
  and need for attention 128–29
  work as form of 236–37
relating, learning about 25

2–3-year-olds 28
4–5-year-olds 30
6–7-year-olds 32
relationships, separation and
divorce 170–71
reproduction 228–29
requests 70–71
resentment, towards parents'
working 236–37
resilience 116–17, 136, 200
restaurants, family friendly 44
rewards
and achievements 173
homework 203
star charts 55, 75, 95, 145
using food as 59
right from wrong 32
rivalry, sibling 124–25
role models 18
appearance 242–43
decision making 47
good manners 188
lying and 143
male role models 139
phones 227, 241
politeness 49
sharing 37, 82
shyness and 63
table manners 43, 45
role play
2–3-year-olds 45, 55, 57, 63,
64–65, 189, 213
4–5-year-olds 31, 107, 122, 151
6–7-year-olds 32, 193, 222
and avoiding physical force 55
boyfriends and girlfriends
222
car journeys 122
eating out 45
feelings 151
friendships 193
good manners 189
moving house 107
phone usage 57
pretend play 64–65
shops and money 212, 213
shyness and 63
rough-and-tumble play 55, 72
routines 87
bedtime 119, 141, 159
dealing with temper tantrums 41, 157
following separation and
divorce 171
moving house 107
rows, sibling 130–31
rules
rule breaking 174–75
tale-telling and 120–21

running 29
running commentaries 28

S

sadness 19, 96, 98, 132–33
safety, temper tantrums and 41
saving money 212, 213
school
after-school activities 244–45
dislike of school 196–97
embarrassing parents 206–207
friendships 190–91, 198–99
homework 14, 75, 173, 182–83, 201,
202–203, 226, 227
illness and 137
pressure of 200–201
school pick-ups 68
self-belief and motivation 220–21
starting new 106, 107
screen time 56–57, 122
screen-free time 217, 226–27
seat belts 122, 161
secrets 235
secure attachments 108–109, 161
"selective attention" 194–95
self-belief 93, 172, 220–1
self-confidence 193
self-consciousness 207, 243
self-control 54, 200
4–5-year-olds 31, 100–101
praising 71
self-criticism 211
self-esteem, humour and 102–103
self-identity, creating positive 85
self-touching 162–63
self-worth 92, 143, 223, 244
building 38, 193
separation anxiety
2–3 year-olds 52–53, 61, 63
4–5 year-olds 90–91
night times 74
separation and divorce 170–71, 214
sequencing 115
serotonin 25
7-year-old development see 6–7 year-old
development
sex education 228–29
shame, feelings of 210–11
sharing
2–3-year-olds 36–37, 54, 82–83
sibling relationships 130
shouting 112–13
show-offs 205
shyness 62–63, 91
siblings
car journeys 122, 123
illness and 136

new additions to the family 134–35
sibling relationships and rivalry
124–25, 130–31, 134–35
tale-telling 121
single parents 15
6–7 year-olds 10, 176–243
after-school activities 245
appearance and physical
perfectionism 242–43
bedtimes 180–81
birthday parties 155
boasting 204–205
boredom 218–19
boyfriends and girlfriends 222–23
car journeys 123
carving out quality time 85
competitive behaviour 224–25
confidence anxieties 182–83
conflicts between parents 214–15
dislike of school 196–97
eating out 45
embarrassing parents 206–207
feelings of shame 210–11
friendships 190–93, 198–99
good manners 189
gratification delay 179
hitting and biting 55
homework 182–83, 201, 202–203
"I hate you" outbursts 184–85
independence 238–39
interrupting 178–79
milestones 32–33
money 212–13
moving home 107
music lessons 230–31
must-have gadgets, toys and clothes
208–209
phones 240–41
playing one parent off the other 186–87
poorly children 137
privacy 234–35
resentment towards parents' working
236–37
school pressure 201
"selective attention" 194–95
self-belief and motivation 220–21
sense of fairness 180–81
separation and divorce 171
sex education 228–29
shyness 63
sleep and bedtimes 75, 216–17, 245
strangers 232–33
technology 227
skills, mastering new 33, 38–39
sleep 74–75
2–3-year-olds 76–77
4–5-year-olds 118–19, 140–41
6–7-year-olds 216–17, 245

bad dreams 140–41
   fear of the dark 118–19
   story time and 76–77
sleepovers 238
snacks 59, 122
social awareness 206–7
social cues 53, 136, 190, 192
social development
   2–3-year-olds 56–57, 62–63, 64–65
   4–5-year-olds 90–91, 146–47
   6–7-year-olds 188–89, 192–93,
      230–31, 239
   music lessons 230–31
   phones and 56–57
   pretend play 64–65
   saying "No" and 239
   shyness and 62–63
   social behaviour 188–89
   social pain 192–93
social rules 30
social skills 44–45, 200
social smarts 191
"special time" 85, 180, 181, 237
speech development
   2–3-year-olds 28
   4–5-year-olds 30
sportsmanship 225
stairs 29
star charts 55, 75, 95, 145
story time 76–77, 107
strangers 60, 232–33
strength and stamina 33
stress 19, 40, 145, 244
stress hormones 25, 99, 211, 214
sucking 94–95
swimming 244

T

table manners 43, 45, 188
tablets 208–209
tact 32
tale-telling 120–21
tantrums
   2–3-year-olds 29, 40–41, 56, 71
   4–5-year-olds 98–99
taxi time 85
teamwork 225, 244
technology
   2–3-year-olds 80–81
   4–5-year-olds 129, 169
   6–7-year-olds 208–209, 216–17, 226–27
   car journeys 122
   curiosity and 80–81
   quality time and 85
telephones
   2–3-year-olds 45, 56–57, 85
   4–5-year-olds 122, 129, 169

6–7-year-olds 226, 240–41
   car journeys 122
   interrupting telephone calls 178–79
   quality time and 85
television 141
temper tantrums
   2–3-year-olds 40–41
   4–5-year-olds 98–99
temperament, empathy and 18
terror attacks 160–61
texture 43
theory of mind 25, 31, 142
thinking milestones 24
   2–3 years 28
   4–5 years 30
   6–7 years 32
3-year-old development see 2–3 year-old
   development
tidying up 148–49
tiger parenting 221
time
   buffer time 79
   car journeys and 122–23
   understanding concept of 86–87
TIY (teach it yourself) 244
toilet humour 103
toilet training
   bedwetting 158–59, 171
   daytime wetting 144–45
toys 208–209
   board games 83, 189, 191, 225
   phones as 56–57
   sharing favourite 36–37, 54
   special toys 126–27
   tidying up 148–49
transitions 68–69
travel, car journeys 122–23
treats
   guilt 170
   repeated asking for 70–71
trust 143
truth telling 142–43
turn-taking 37, 189, 191
2–3-year-old development 10, 34–87
   after-school activities 245
   birthday parties 155
   books 76–77
   'bossiness' 48–49
   car journeys 123
   carving out quality time 85
   childcare 52–53, 60–61
   confidence 72
   curiosity 80–81
   decision making 46–47, 50–51
   disrupting or ending play 68–69
   eating out 45
   exploration 78–79
   food battles 58–59

fussy eaters 42–43
   good manners 189
   gratification delay 66–67, 87
   hitting and biting 54–55
   impatience 86–87
   independence 38–39, 50–51, 69
   memory development 77
   milestones 28–29
   money 212–13
   moving home 107
   phones 56–57
   poorly children 137
   preferring one parent to another
      72–73
   pretend play 64–65
   requests for things 70–71
   school pressure 201
   separation anxiety 52–53, 61, 63
   separation and divorce 171
   sharing 36–37, 82–83
   shyness 63
   sleep 75
   tantrums 40–41, 71
   technology 227
   transitions 68–69
   vocabulary 77

U

understanding, development of 38, 30, 32
uniqueness 200
urinary tract infections 144

V

values 16–17, 143, 209
vegetables 42, 43
video games 119, 141, 216–17
vocabulary
   2–3-year-olds 28, 29, 47, 77
   4–5-year-olds 30, 110
   6–7-year-olds 32

W

waiting 66–67
walking 29, 79
websites 226–27
wellbeing, emotional 18–19, 193, 200
wetting, daytime 144–45
whining 71, 84
Winnicott, Donald 20
winning and losing 224–25
wishful thinking 71
work, child's resentment towards 236–37
worries 75
   worry gremlins 197
   see also anxiety; fears

THE AUTHOR

Tanith Carey is an award-winning UK journalist and author who writes on the most pressing challenges facing today's parents. Her eight previous books have been translated into 15 languages, including German, French, Arabic, Chinese, Korean and Turkish. Having spent time working in the US as an editor and writer before returning to the UK, Tanith has insight on both sides of the Atlantic and her writing has featured in a wide range of publications, including the *Daily Telegraph*, *The Times*, *The Guardian*, and *New York Daily News*. Tanith also appears on TV and radio programmes, such as *NBC Today* in the US, Radio 4's *Woman's Hour* and *You and Yours*, ITV's *This Morning*, the *Lorraine show*, and *Good Morning Britain*. Tanith has two daughters (16 and 13).

THE CONSULTANT

Dr Angharad Rudkin is a Clinical Psychologist and Associate Fellow of the British Psychological Society. She has worked with children, adolescents, and families for over 15 years. Angharad has an independent therapy practice and teaches Clinical Child Psychology at the University of Southampton. She regularly contributes to articles on child and family wellbeing for national newspapers and magazines, and is a relationship expert for London's *Metro* daily paper. Angharad appears on TV and radio regularly as an expert on child and family issues.

ACKNOWLEDGMENTS

From the author Thanks to my children Lily and Clio who made this possible. This is the book I was looking for when you were small and hope you will find it insightful if you have your own children. I learned from you both. Also love to my husband Anthony whose support allowed me to take the time to write this book. A special mention must also go to wonderful agent Caroline Montgomery and, of course, Dr Angharad Rudkin, my calm, wise and always reasonable consultant, whose first priority has always been to help parents understand their children better. Finally, it's not easy to produce a parenting book that is truly original, but which is also as accessible and user-friendly as this one – and the London DK staff behind this project have been fantastic. What a team.

From the consultant Thank you Gwenda and Arthur for wrapping up my childhood with such love and belief, and thank you to David, Nora, Bridget and Arthur who have taught me more than any textbook could.

From the publisher We would like to acknowledge the following in the production of this book: Kathy Steer for proofreading and Vanessa Bell for indexing.